A
THEOLOGY
OF
AUSCHWITZ

The Christian Faith
and the Problem of Evil

Ulrich Simon

John Knox Press
ATLANTA

First published in Great Britain 1967
by Victor Gollancz Ltd

First published in paperback in 1978
by SPCK
Holy Trinity Church
Marylebone Road
London NW1 4DU

BT
160
S54
1979

ISBN 0-8042-0724-0

First published in the United States of America in 1979
by John Knox Press, Atlanta, Georgia

Printed in the United States of America

CONTENTS

TO THE MEMORY OF
GEORGE BELL
Bishop of Chichester, 1929–58
AND
VICTOR GOLLANCZ
who perceived and fought
the great evil

I

PREFACE

THEOLOGY IS THE science of divine reality, Auschwitz (Oswiecim) is a place in Poland where millions of
human beings were killed between 1942 and 1945. This
Konzentrationslager occupied about fifteen square miles
and consisted of three main and thirty-nine subsidiary
camps. The first prisoner arrived on July 14th, 1940.
The camp was evacuated and for the most part destroyed
by January 27th, 1945, before Russian troops liberated
what was left of it. There were only 40,000 registered
prisoners among the millions who perished there without
leaving a name.

At first sight Theology and Auschwitz have nothing in
common. The former articulates a joyful tradition, the
latter evokes the memory of untold suffering. Theology
speaks of eternal light, Auschwitz perpetuates the horror
of darkness. Nevertheless, as light and darkness are com-
plementary in our experience, and as the Glory and the
shame must be apprehended together, so the momentous
outrage of Auschwitz cannot be allowed to stand, as it
has done, in an isolation such as the leprous outcast used
to inspire in the past. 'The evils that men do live after
them'; unless they are understood they may recur.

Such an understanding meets with endless obstacles.
It is easy enough to present the documentation of what
happened in Auschwitz between 1942 and 1945. The

facts, which will only briefly figure here, are available to all who care to open the files.[1] The lawyers have put us in their debt by enabling us to see the scene of unprecedented crime in as unemotional light as possible. The pictures of the tormented, the dying, and the dead, as well as of the death factories, have become the exhibits in the many trials which have been held to bring guilty men to justice. The subject has thus been frozen with the unemotional air of the dispassionate procedure of justice. These cases were listed, heard, and concluded under criminal law.

This documentation, however, is also supplemented by the books and records of the witnesses who belong to the very small number of survivors.[2] Even the dead have left a few final jottings and pictures which have been found and collected. Thus we need not rely exclusively upon judicial material. We may heed the voices of the still living and of the dead.

The theologian's task is not to infuse into the subject the ingredient of sensationalism of which the law-courts have deprived it, nor to repress the deep feelings which the voices from the past stir in our hearts. The theologian will approach Auschwitz with a self-imposed discipline equal to that of the lawyer, sacrificing nothing of the

---

[1] *Trials of Major War Criminals: Proceedings of the International Military Tribunal at Nuremberg*, 22 vols., 1946–51; *United Nations, War Crimes Commissions, Law Reports of Trials of War Criminals*, 14 vols., 1947–9; The War Trial Series; K. Smolem, *Auschwitz*, 1961; G. Reitlinger, *The Final Solution*, 1953.

The Wiener Library, London, contains the fullest documentation of all kinds.

Cf. also transcripts of the German Auschwitz trial of 1965.

[2] e.g., Primo Levi, *If This is a Man*, 1962.

clarity which the judicial approach affords. He will also observe the reticence of a pilgrim to a place of martyrdom.

The theologian's enquiry goes beyond the terms of criminal investigation and the sifting of evidence. Unlike the court he is not satisfied by the elucidation of the facts. He must ask the great 'Why?', rather than be content to know how and when certain crimes were perpetrated. He extends the 'Why?' to the root of the historical drama and to the actors in it. He will compare and contrast his findings with the declared Christian doctrines. How does Auschwitz stand in the light of the Fatherhood of God, the Person and Work of Christ, and the Coming of the Holy Ghost? These norms of Christian theology govern our enquiry and rule out an untidy or hysterical survey. They exclude a morbid fascination with facts which the human eye finds too repulsive to see and which the mind cannot fathom.

Yet these theological norms are not an excuse to blur the facts. We are dealing with the deaths of millions, mostly non-combatant Jews, who had been rounded up and sent to various concentration-camps designed entirely for their extermination. Auschwitz was the largest but by no means the only place of infamy. At Treblinka, Maideneck, Ravensbrück, Dachau, Buchenwald, Belsen, Chelmno, Sohibor, Mauthausen and many lesser known places the same dimensions of sin and suffering prevailed. Auschwitz stands here for the whole guilt which has stained the earth, not only in Europe but also in Asia.

This guilt must in the first place be ascribed to Hitler, the German Chancellor from 1933 until his death by suicide, probably on April 30th, 1945, in Berlin. He appointed the men who carried out the task of extermination with ruthless efficiency. The details of the design, administration, and final dissolution of these camps belong to history and are not directly relevant to our concern. We are, however, directly concerned with the ministers, executives, commanders, and ordinary men and women who carried out Hitler's orders. The clash between the guilty and their innocent victims spurs us on to our theological task.

Auschwitz belongs to the past, thank God. But its multi-dimensional range of evil extends to the present and throws its shadow over the future. It is for our purpose the comprehensive and realistic symbol of the greatest possible evil which still threatens mankind. A theology of Auschwitz is, therefore, an attempt to interpret this evil responsibly for the present.

Since the above was written, the following important books have appeared: A. Kaplan, *Scroll of Agony;* J. F. Steiner, *Treblinka;* Gideon Hausner, *Justice in Jerusalem;* Bern Naumann, *Auschwitz;* Norman Cohn, *Warrant for Genocide;* Pierre d'Harcourt, *The Real Enemy.* For the legal problems involved see, for example, G. Schwarzenberger, *The Eichmann Judgment,* Current Legal Problems, 1962.

THE CONFLICT

THE NEED FOR the present investigation is not felt by all. The generation which was too young to have any share in, or did not even exist to be connected with, Auschwitz cannot be expected to wish to penetrate the .abyss. Even those who were not too young and did have a share in these events prefer the present normalcy to the revival of unwanted memories. Theologians, too, stress the Here and Now as our main concern to the exclusion of the past.

Yet this turning away from one of the greatest human tragedies is neither wise nor moral. The dangers which threaten our own society arise out of ills which lie in that past. They have remained uncured, and it is in the interest of civilized normality to lay bare the secrets of these ills so that they may be rendered less menacing.

But this sociological obligation cannot alone guide theological reasoning. It has its own tradition of sin, guilt, expiation, propitiation, and atonement. These difficult terms should not, however, serve to darken counsel. What the Christian theologian must explain, if he can, is not only why there is evil and suffering in the world, which God has created and sustains and directs with his power, but why these ills are not wholly worthless. If he can show the pattern of Christ's sacrifice, which summarizes all agonies, as the reality behind

Auschwitz he fulfils his obligation to the Here and Now.

Such an endeavour is no theoretical exercise in words. Guilt is not purged by words, nor suffering made tolerable by fine phrases. There is, rightly, a moral resistance to making Auschwitz acceptable, and Christians must be careful not to speak rashly of atonement and reconciliation, especially because grave doubts remain whether all Christian institutions did all in their power to mitigate the horrors of the 'final solution'.[1] This burden of the past is seen by some as a moral reason for the present decline in Christian institutions. We need not give our assent to this claim whilst we maintain that atonement for Auschwitz has become a matter of life and death for Christianity.

Some may object, however, that the political past should not obtrude on theology. It is perfectly true that doctrine cannot be altered according to the passing fancies of an age. The last thing that we should want is to create a 'Face of God after Auschwitz',[2] for such a face could be no more than another man-made image cast in the furnace of despair.

The experience of political evil is the very stuff of Christian theology. The story of what Austin Farrar calls 'Love Almighty and Ills Unlimited',[3] comes to man

---

[1] Hochhuth's indictment of Pope Pius XII in *The Representative*, exaggerated as it is in parts, remains unanswered and unanswerable. Cf. Saul Friedländer, *Pius XII and the Third Reich*, 1966.

[2] Notwithstanding this misleading title, Ignaz Maybaum's book of this title (1965) is to be welcomed as an attempt, on the Jewish side, to connect the *churban* with traditional doctrine. Despite flashes of insight, however, the book is marred by repetitive passages and a disappointing misconception of Christianity.

[3] Published 1962.

through the reading of history, first of Israel and then of Christ and his Church. The Babylonian Exile, the spoliation of the Temple, the Crucifixion, the Fall of Jerusalem, are links on the continuous chain of events which, despite, or because of, its catastrophic import, grants us the insight into God's dealings with man which nature and speculation cannot supply.

Auschwitz must, therefore, be seen against the canvas of tradition, even if, as we maintain, a new element of evil will have to be comprehended. Auschwitz can be seen to recapitulate the impressive array of all the ills as they were known to Christian theology before 1942. The hostility of the forces of nature, such as heat and cold, drought and rain, wind and snow; the rule of accident and chance, as manifested in the grotesque 'order' of the camp; the war between man and other life, such as dogs and insects; the alienation between groups, classes, nations, races, generations—all these and more destructive forces, open or hidden, general or particular, contributed to the climax of lawlessness of which pain, agony, death, decomposition, and cremation may be cited as the apex of an incontestable logic of evil.

Auschwitz gives a new note to this tradition by removing from it every vestige of theory. In general our natural reaction to pain succeeds in reducing the ache to manageable proportions. We seek to be spectators without being involved in loss. We know that until it happens to be my pain, or it is 'my son Absalom' whose death I lament, we can erect castles in the air against the reality of suffering. Remote plagues, earthquakes, explosions, or wrecked ships do not touch our existential core. But this disaster, once grasped in its immensity, tolls the bell for the whole world. Its impact is that of a personal bereavement, which, as C. S. Lewis showed with a searing insight, spells out the end of theories.

It may be held that the human mechanism of self-protection still continues to operate now as before. Yet against this view must be set the knowledge that this mechanism is faulty. Now, it may be argued, no excuse for self-willed blindness remains. These events have certainly stripped from apologetic theology all the cheaper brands of consolation. Gone, for example, is the pleasing theory, once even entertained by C. S. Lewis,[1] that the quantity of suffering can have no bearing on the problem of pain since we suffer as individuals. On the contrary, Auschwitz disposes of evil and suffering as a kind of private issue. It affirms the ancient tradition that in the corporate affront to God, the violation of his rule, the universal disease, individual experience of suffering is inescapably only a part of an infinitely greater whole.

Now the traditional arguments, which have been put forward in the past to justify God's ways with man, have never given complete, or even a great deal of, satisfaction. These so-called theodicies endeavoured to rationalize the irrational. Under the glaring light of a concentration camp they still command respect, if only by pinpointing the nature of the conflict.

We must first pass in review the ancient theory that suffering is the result of sin. It can be supported by a host of texts, is not confined to Christian thinking, but may almost be said to come from any market-place. It is the slogan of a healthy common-sense: 'as a man sows, so

[1] *A Grief Observed*, 1961, makes up for some of the deficiencies of *The Problem of Pain*, 1940.

shall he reap'. The formula x sin = x suffering states not only the cause and effect but also the content of sin and suffering in proportionate terms.

Our survey of Auschwitz confirms that a law of cause and effect governs sin and suffering. It must also acknowledge that degrees of suffering exist and that these are related to the degree of evil intended and performed. For example, even in the general greyness of unutterable gloom greater shades of horror must be attributed to certain outrageous institutions, such as the punishment blocks.

On other counts, however, the calculation fails. Here the agent of sin certainly does not suffer for his own sin, except possibly in ways which he would not register as suffering. The prophets in the Old Testament had already seen that the victims suffer for another's sins. The teaching and the example of Christ ruled out a crude rule of thumb by which to measure any man's share in sin by assessing his suffering. The formula x sin = x suffering had to be dismissed even then as an absurd simplification.

The picture which we are forced to look at is highly complex, not only because the victims are clearly not reaping their own, but other men's, rewards, but also because the content of the sin cannot be measured. We can no longer speak conveniently of recognizable deadly sins, since gluttony, covetousness, lust, envy, anger, sloth, and pride—though never far absent—do not explain, or account for, the total indifference or sadistic pleasure which prevailed in the camp.

The absence of a measurable crime was noted in particular when the war-criminals were tried before the courts. The question at issue could never be, as in ancient laws, that of fixing the amount of guilt so that the accused could make restitution to his victims or their legal heirs. This procedure has in any case become impossible in serious cases. But in dealing with war crimes all punishments seemed irrelevant just because the nature of the evil could not be assessed in a normal manner. Even the sentences that were passed could hardly be regarded as deterrents, let alone as means of restitution, reparation, or satisfaction.

Yet these trials also brought out a positive revaluation of the moral conflict. The court could not arrogate for itself the office of God, or of a Supreme Being, and weigh up the immeasurable proportions of sin and suffering. But the judges gave expression to the commonly felt conviction that, so far as humanly possible, justice cannot remain passive alongside unatoned and unexpiated outrages. Thus the judges stressed on many occasions that human retribution, though wholly inadequate, pertained to the very function of justice, even when face to face with an intrinsically impossible case. Even if the execution of a commander of Auschwitz may not deter future commanders from committing similar attrocities, and brings satisfaction to no one, it shows, if only by articulating the impotence of the law, the imperishable challenge of the moral law and its vindication.

This legal approach never failed to stress that the point of the accusation, and thus of the conflict, concerned not so much the nature of the offence but the degree of responsibility to be attached to the accused. The defence, quite rightly, seized upon this point as vital. The theologian, too, must find in the degrees of freedom a key to the multi-dimensional chaos of evil at Auschwitz. What matters to us—since nothing can now be altered—is who did what to whom, and why, and with what degree of accountability.

This multi-dimensional view helps us to come to closer quarters with the problem of the nature of evil itself. It takes us out of the world of bazaars, where one thing is changed for another (so much sin, so much suffering), and opens to us the vast universe of human relationships. Auschwitz may warn us not to go too far in this respect, for in that infernal world material things matter almost more than relationships, for a piece of bread keeps alive, whereas friendship may not. But even this realistic note reinforces the paramount question: What is evil? Is it a real thing? To what extent is Auschwitz real? Is it not its unreality which is its evil? It is not for nothing that so many prisoners despaired of understanding it and admonished themselves not even to seek a rational explanation.

In many classical theodicies the so-called privative view of evil is held. It maintains that ultimately all evil is a deficiency, an absence of being, the denial of God. This view has also often been caricatured by its enemies, if only by quoting the frivolous example of the ordinary tooth-ache which, it is said, is real enough and the bane of every moral philosopher. In fact, the tooth-ache can be cited to support the theory, for it is not the tooth which is evil, nor the nerve which communicates and whose ends register the pain. The cavity causes the conditions of the pain, but it is not the pain, though it is the seat of the evil. It may, therefore, be argued that the pain is a good thing, for it draws attention to defective organisms.

Similarly, the pain may have a positive quality and draw attention to the absence of the good.

To a certain extent Auschwitz endorses some aspects of this privative view of evil. Its only point is to cause death, and it is therefore essentially meaningless in terms of life. It is the infamous illustration to the world that this is the way to create a no-world, a tangle of wire and a morass. The complete absence of sense and decency, however, cogently urges minimum virtues as the basis of human existence. The pain and the residuum of guilt will have helped to create a better atmosphere to blot out other social evils. Thus the privations of Auschwitz may be subsequently compensated for by meaningful goodness.

The attractions of this theory, in which evil is not only a deficient but also an effective good, never fail to meet with popular esteem. To say, for example, that Auschwitz represented the absence of reality then, and now inspires Israel and the world with a high conception of statesmanship, is by no means beside the point. But unfortunately this reading of the matter does not cut the edge of the evil. If this combined theory fails miserably even in ordinary cases of bereavement, losses and accidents of all kinds, how much more must it ring hollow and somehow coldly shabby when we are confronted with the arena which history displays.

Our refusal to be enticed by this comfortable doctrine is not only induced by an emotional dissent. Since the days of Voltaire the very words 'all things, including evil, are for the best in the best of all possible worlds' sound like a parody. The pre-established harmony, which Leibnitz set forth in his system, could never recover from the malicious blows which Voltaire meted out to Professor Pangloss (= Leibnitz) in his satirical *Candide*. Even at this stage of history it is a wholesome medicine for any privationist to read this lampoon to be cured from his belief by making the long journey through a series of misfortunes.

But we are not concerned with fiction and we shall seek to show that Auschwitz is partly the product of this ill-fated optimism, which would spirit away evil, sickness, and death by pretending that they are not there, because horrors on such a scale are unthinkable. Theologians have in any case never subscribed to this form of self-hypnotism. Although an optimistic approach is perhaps endemic to all theorizers about evil, their belief that all things are working together for good stems from belief in God, who not only condemns and annihilates evil, but also overcomes it by his own work in redemption.

By placing evil within an eternal framework we leave behind illusory self-deception. By introducing a time-scale beyond human experience we grant the phenomenon of temporal evil in history its full claims to reality. By postulating the existence of a spiritual universe we believe the moral distinction between good and evil to reach beyond the sphere of historical happenings. Thus theology has always given the problem a subtle place in metaphysical thinking.

Nevertheless, the shadow of Auschwitz falls upon this apologia and darkens the otherworldly conception inherent in it. To a certain extent the book of Job already anticipates our suspicion that this answer, too, is too easy an answer. Job pours bitter irony on the doctrine that a good God can cause the innocent to suffer. The simplicity of the argument, indignantly reiterated to the point of exhaustion, protests especially against metaphysical otherworldliness. Man is neither a stone, i.e., insensitive and invulnerable, nor an angelic spirit. On the contrary, it is precisely in time and space and through his body that man suffers. All consolations which ignore this point are beside the point. The nature of the conflict demands another solution. Job is the spokesman not of the atheists, but of the believers, for he brushes aside all subsidiary considerations, such as fortune and misfortune, accident and chance. God is the author of evil and responsible for it. Just because God is good and omnipotent there is no point in looking for a solution elsewhere. Man is accountable to God, but God is also accountable to man.

We cannot here trace the whole drama of Job and need not accept, or reject, its message as a whole. The survivor of Auschwitz is content to probe the problem with the same dialectic. It establishes the tradition which looks not only to a number of laws and natural causes, nor places evil in a timeless system beyond, but begins with God as the creator of the human condition, of which human suffering is so essential a part.

Such a dialectic, however, soon leaves behind the somewhat childish monism, which the author of the book of Job imputes to his hero. It would be absurd in the light of our quest to put God in the dock as the direct agent of an immoral order. Even in the book of Job, as it now stands, such a grotesque step is skilfully avoided, for in the prologue of the book we are told in the form of a fable that Satan acts by God's permission. His malicious advocacy is, of course, known to us only, so that Job and his interlocutors speak in ignorance of what their readers know well.

Our concern, however, is not with this literary finesse but with the consequent thought which is taken seriously in those theological circles which wish to vindicate God's ways with men. Develop the theme of Satan, and you have an enemy, of God, of goodness, of mankind. Call it the serpent, or the evil principle, or the tempter, or the accuser, seducer, or what you like—Beliar, devil, Apollyon—and you somehow begin to shift the load. The conflict is now both more understandable and more mysterious, for the divine power is opposed by another, hostile to God and man, thus putting man in God's camp as an ally.

We have no wish to present here any of the different computations of this dualistic development of thought. Tradition, it is true, resists an absolute and stark dualism —as, for example, between light and darkness—in as much as the Enemy is never allowed to rank as god. Yet the conflict is real enough, as depicted by Milton in *Paradise Lost*. Satan and the fallen angels still owe their existence to God, but in rebelling they temporarily undermine his sovereignty, thus engulfing men in a cosmic war.

This modified dualism, which frankly proclaims the Lord's battle, has the advantage of exonerating God. He neither makes nor condones evil, though he permits its manifestation in the interest of freedom. God is not the supreme sadist who vivisects his creatures, but he sides with them in the tremendous undertaking of creating perfect love. Without this hypothesis it would be impossible to maintain that God is good and powerful. The

Christian claim that it pleased God to redeem the world by his Son's death could not have been substantiated at all.

But in the context of human history and scientific knowledge it is extremely difficult to apply a notion of conflict which, on the surface at least, does not seem at all to square with experience. Even in antiquity the great masters had to go to elaborate lengths to accommodate their peculiar problems to so transcendental a thesis as the Kingdom of God. If men like Augustine and Dante finally succeeded in bending their earthly observations to their celestial convictions it was due, one feels, not so much to the facts as to their genius which re-created them.

However successful these mental acrobatics may have been in the past the modern temper has for a long time declined to take them seriously for any practical purpose. The mystery of evil has been put into cold storage. The pious man is content to say, and perhaps to believe, that certain evils are sent to try him, i.e., to test his integrity. He cannot say who sends them, even if he submits. The less pious man hates even this last residue of mythical thinking, and Auschwitz certainly has nothing in it to confirm a myth. When the world was young, the gods did not scruple to try their followers in ordeals. They fought each other and the humans reflected their battles, as, for example, outside Troy. But even centuries before Christ the philosophers exploded the engaging naivety of these myths and rejected the belief in a tragic conflict above, to account for our miserable necessity below.

After Auschwitz we meet with a common resolution to abandon everything remotely connected with mythology. We must see and apprehend the conflict in its factual light. But the result of our front against all mythical tight-rope walking is not without its own dangers, for it induces a simple, sceptical silence. Even orthodox Christian thought once talked, and still talks, of the 'mystery' of evil, implying thereby that nothing useful can really be said on the subject. We may now go further and drop the word 'mystery' and give no explanation of our ills because we are convinced that there is none. As Job observed centuries ago, without being refuted, we are in a world which cares not for our well-being. The mountains and the sea are notorious for their silence. Some men take heavy knocks while others escape, but only for a time.

Yet this scepticism, too, remains intolerable when we walk over the camp to-day. Perhaps it may even be the root of our ills, for it paves the way to that moral relativism which suspends all judgments of right and wrong and thereby sustains the rule of terror. A belief in the rule of chance, coupled with that in the survival of the fittest and made respectable by our awareness of the almost endless varieties of customs among the peoples of the world, creates the mentality which understands, condones, and pardons all. Viewed in this light the conflict tends to be relegated to an issue of regional preferences and local climate.

It can hardly be denied that this so-called liberal substitute for traditional theodicy is one of the causes of Auschwitz. Paradoxically this hell was the last thing that any progressive thinkers ever intended. But their ideology came to buttress the slogan 'Everything is permitted'. Even in the nineteenth century Dostoevsky showed, especially in *Crime and Punishment* and in *The Devils*, that by blurring the dividing line between right and wrong and condoning criminal nihilism by means of psychological sympathy, the well-meaning encourage and finally help to establish the power of criminals and demons. When 'everything is permitted' any student may dream of becoming a Napoleon and may consequently justify the killing of a hoarding miser to pay his way. Every aspirant to power may trap and kill his adversary, since the means justifies the end, all being free to pursue their urges. Thus Dostoevsky's well-meaning and engaging Stepan Trofimovich in *The Devils*, lover of academic freedom and literary liberalism (shades of Turgeniev), upholder of every humanist ideal, is the father of the terrorist Pyotr, who, bereft of conscience and scruples of any kind, would have been only too happy in command at Auschwitz.

This breakdown of the liberal ethic is not a matter of fiction but highlights the nature of the conflict. Auschwitz was its logical consequence and physical apex. The serious contention that 'all things are lawful' was there seriously carried out. Auschwitz demonstrates the deadly potency of a moral relativism which attracts Christian theologians in their flirtation with the world. Even in the post-Auschwitz era the demand for toleration in all things can be discerned as the precursor to new forms of terrorism. It asks for, and obtains, theological sanction for a new morality which is tailored to all the destructive instincts. Thus the sincerity of progressive reformers enhances the peril to the world and to themselves.

The particular danger of this abuse of tolerance lies in the acceptance of evil as a natural phenomenon. One might almost say that the conflict ceases to be one once it is deprived of a court of appeal. Even Auschwitz can, humanly speaking, be interpreted as a simple clash of interests, a murder story with one code for the victors, and another for the vanquished. Goering knew this only too well when he boasted of a 'double standard of morality'. He has his heirs among those who regard man as a law unto himself and freely embrace such a positive analysis of, and apology for, extermination. If the weak meet with the strong in war and suffer their final defeat, who can gainsay the law of the strong?

The enlightened conscience, however, utters its protest against this ruthless realism. It is not entirely without weapons. The defeat of Hitler not only enables this voice to make itself heard against all tyranny, but it has evidence enough to prove that Hitlerism was defeated because of its outrageous immorality. But even this is not enough to clinch the matter, for having once sanctioned criminality, though unwittingly, humanism lacks the categories of judgment by which it can repudiate evil on a transcendent scale.

The lasting significance of Auschwitz for humanity lies in its disclosure of the human condition as something incomprehensible and insoluble in merely human terms. The conflict occurred on a dimension which cannot be understood according to any theories or myths. But before we approach this dimension, and invoke its moral authority, we must take a closer look at the tangible, earthly evidence.

III

THE PROBLEM AND ITS INTERPRETATION

Between us and Auschwitz lies a wide gulf. It evokes all the intellectual problems which historians and theologians know only too well. The complexity of the facts makes an objective selection impossible. As a phenomenon it belongs to the history of the Second World War and must be understood as part of its political, economic, and military course.

The problem, however, is greater than our understanding of the course of history. The peculiar nature of Auschwitz raises the problem of man. The 'face of man' after Auschwitz looks ambiguous. The masters and the victims of Auschwitz do not, in the first place, articulate the old questions about man, with which philosophers and theologians have been familiar for centuries, such as: Is man made in the image of God? Is his destiny meaningful or not? Is he made for eternity or not? All these questions seem a trifle unreal when face to face with the squads of laughing torturers and the sick, dirty, smelly, defenceless, dishonoured 'muslims' (as the condemned and selected were called). The criminals as well as the innocent solicit, not only revenge on the one hand, and pity on the other, but an enquiry into the nature of the human kind.

This enquiry must raise the problem of our own involvement in that historical situation. We have neither gassed, nor been gassed, and stand outside the whole horrible thing. On the other hand we share the 'banality'[1] of the guards, with their family cares, ordinary talents and tastes. Similarly we depend upon a minimum of living conditions to keep us from falling into the pit. We are, therefore, potentially part of the dishonouring and the dishonoured humanity and cannot answer 'What is Man?' without comparing the phenomena of Auschwitz with our own physical and spiritual make-up.

This tentative identification enables us to turn the historical sketch into an existentialist enquiry. Hence the emotional reaction belongs to the proper study, and if we protest against an anthropology of despair, based upon the sight of heaps of skeletons and smoking furnaces, and press for a vindication of mankind, a restatement of meaning and destiny, it is based upon a belief reacting to these facts.

It is, therefore, our interpretation of the problem which connects Auschwitz with 'sacred history', i.e., that ideology which detects meaning behind the meaningless, by such categories as creation, salvation, redemption. We are bold enough to apply the very terms of thought which, on the face of it, Auschwitz has banished, just as the Evangelists, for example, looked at the gibbet and derived from that sight the good news of Christ crucified. Such a reading back into an event is obviously perilous, since it may go against the evidence of ascertainable events. But given the proper reticence it may become the creative, spiritual conquest of the bare facts.

Such a 'sacred history', however, demands a knowledge of the causes which produced this culmination of

[1] Cf. Hannah Arendt's controversial *Eichmann in Jerusalem*, 1963.

corporate terror. We may dismiss from the start the notion that the human order is so capriciously arranged that things happen simply because they happen. It may be argued that there is a rhythm in which violence and destruction succeed to peace and progress, but we cannot hang our whole historical development on a wheel of fortune to be fatalistically accepted. Nor can a crude evolutionary theory account for our human condition as examined here. The animality of our nature does not constitute our problem, which is one of men caught up in a scientific civilization.

Yet there is a new primitiveness in the scientific context which characterizes our humanity. It is known by its fervour and infective solidarity. The group's enthusiasm stamps out effective individualism. It recalls the intoxicating technique of mantic and hysteria. The rhythm of music, the acceleration of movement, the repetitive chanting of slogans, induce a state of mind in which men deem themselves invulnerable to ordinary restraints and dangers. Conventions, criticisms, and appeals to reason diminish and finally vanish before a power which possesses the possessed. The ensuing quasi-religious ecstasy of the masses, and their communion in this ecstatic state, must be regarded as the first and essential step in the escalation which leads to the explosive violence and systematic murder of human beings outside the ecstatic circle.

Although there were cynics among the leading SS officers—lawyers, for the most part, who were quite above the mob psychosis—Auschwitz is unthinkable apart from enthusiastic, religious ecstasy. The problem, therefore, is to establish the inner connection between the charismatic totalitarianism and the holocaust of innocent beings.

Unfortunately the existent psychological answers do but rarely satisfy. What the criminals have vouchsafed to tell us, such as Hoess, commander of Auschwitz, throws practically no light upon their motivation. It is true that some of these case histories are interesting and sound like those of ordinary criminals. We hear of illegitimate sons, fatherless boys whose fathers had fallen in the First World War, of all sorts of failures and human wrecks. Occasionally there is evidence of sexual troubles, deviations, and sadistic practices. But on the whole Hannah Arendt's judgment must stand that these men were as banal as the rest of the world's little men. What she underestimates is the impact of the charismatic upon such men, who long to escape from their autistic, self-imprisoning solitude. They were not like the tormented souls whom we meet on the pages of Kafka or Dostoevsky or Strindberg, but they responded to a 'call'. Their ecstatic possibility afforded relief first, and power later.

If this is a true assessment, the cause of Auschwitz cannot be confined to the religious charisma, to which Hitler appealed with unbelievable success, but must include the whole situation. This is not just another case of the priority of the chicken or the egg. Rather we face here the problem of the interpenetration of the ecstatic state and its scope in the world. As we know, most ecstasies remain private and leave not a trace in the world. The abnormal feature preceding Auschwitz is the readiness of the seed-bed to receive such a seed.

The complex and broken-down economy of the late 1920's provided that seed-bed. The facts have been

narrated too often to be repeated here:[1] inflation, depression, mass unemployment, chimneys without smoke,
hearths without coal, bellies without food, wheat and
coffee burnt, the wave of bankruptcies, suicides, a world-
wide crisis of confidence—these things favoured a revolutionary solution.

The economic chaos was the seed-bed, not the seed.
The loss of the war, and then the loss of property, produced a genuine anxiety even in the least criminal circles.
Good men and women wished to preserve a godly
heritage. They feared the Marxist class-struggle and
looked for a barrier against the bored and despairing
millions who marched under the Red Flag. But nothing
could happen until the fears of the dispossessed and the
fervour of the have-nots could be united, financed, and
marshalled into one aggressively vindictive longing for
compensation. A ruling class, which senses its decline,
and a working class, which finds no work, cannot be
mobilized into one revolutionary force except through a
religious ecstasy, and this seed Hitler could provide.

His hatred of the Jews was, as he well knew, the lever
by which to turn the potential into an actual *levée en
masse*. Here was the longed-for common ecstatic denominator, which combined tradition with revolution in
a social bond. History had singled out the Jewish people
for a special role.

After the First World War the Jews' position in Germany had improved and many of them had become
prominent in the highest positions. During the inflation
some had made remarkable fortunes almost overnight.

[1] For the best account cf. W. S. Churchill, *The Second World War*,
vol. 1.

THE PROBLEM AND ITS INTERPRETATION 33

When others had become 'poor' they had become 'rich'. This lucky minority—with which the millions in Poland and Russia had nothing in common since their economic status deteriorated all the time—founded new industries and owned a share in stores, banks, breweries, textile factories, etc. Their success was not at first resented, but as the depression pursued its cankerous growth, it became the target of militant envy. As Hannah Arendt rightly diagnoses, the concentration of wealth, without an adequate share in responsible government and power, gives the green light to the disgruntled to attempt a gigantic take-over of that wealth. Its stages are expropriation, exile, and murder.[1]

Yet the political exploitation of this economic situation demanded that the impersonal be geared into a flame of personal, ecstatic hatred. Hitler came to regard the Jewish question as the lynch-pin of his aspirations. He saw the Jews as the living witnesses of a long tradition. If the tradition was to go then the witnesses had to be annihilated. Thus he gave a theological twist to the politico-economic aims.

The history of Anti-Semitism is the history of the Jews since the destruction of Jerusalem in A.D. 70 and is therefore inseparable from Christian theology. What Hitler came to achieve had been prefigured theologically, for the Jews had become the enemies of the Cross and partly identified with Anti-Christ. Jewish religion, Jewish customs, and Jewish existence as such, were felt to be an affront on theological grounds. The miraculous survival of Israel outside the land of Israel was not generally considered a divine favour and evidence of a

[1] Cf. Hannah Arendt, *The Burden of our Time*, 1951.

providential design. The eternal Jew walked over the earth as a curse, and the expulsions, crusades, pogroms, and ghettoes, were an everlasting reminder of its reality. They were a demonstration of God's displeasure, the retribution to Judas for his treacherous kiss.

But even the anti-Semitic theology of the Church did not prevent kings and popes from protecting 'their' Jews and limiting the ground-swell of popular resentment and the Jew-baiting with its fantastic mythology. The lower classes fancied the tales of baby-sacrificing and blood-drinking Jews, veritable ogres who indulged in magic and cannibalism, whilst the upper classes despised this nonsense. Thus there developed a theological underworld of propaganda which flourished particularly in times of failing harvests and economic crises.[1] No doubt Anti-Semitism was one certain way of rousing the mob to the feverish pitch of enthusiasm. Yet this enthusiasm, though theologically underpinned, was by its very nature local and short-lived. It did not effect a total extermination.

When feudal rule yielded to bourgeois capitalism a new era began for the Jews, which culminated later in the advent of Napoleon and the emancipation in Western Europe during the nineteenth century. At first it seemed that the new threat to the Jews would come from their loss of identity through gradual assimilation. Even a mass conversion to Christianity seemed imminent, if only for reasons of liberal sentiment and adjustment. Later still, the Marxist revolution with its aim of the abolition of religion and classes, and its share of Jewish supporters, seemed to proclaim the end of persecutions. With world brotherhood on the threshold

[1] Cf. Norman Cohn, *The Pursuit of the Millenium*, 1957.

the Jewish question seemed practically settled. To many Jews Zionism seemed no longer necessary.

But the theological rumbling never ceased. Protestant theologians from the time of the Reformation clung to the inherited tradition of the new Israel and consequently denounced the old.[1] Even on the lower level of local church-papers and little Bible- and prayer-papers there remained an agreed anti-semitic method of exposition which was all the more powerful in its being taken for granted. When liberal, and presently socialist, ideas came to be known as inimical to Christian interests, and, furthermore, suspected of unpatriotic motives and Jewish support, this theological undercurrent was ready to break out into a flood. Thus the Dreyfus case in France (1894–1906) split the country, and presently Europe, into Jew-haters and their opponents. The former were no longer the poor and the rabble, but, on the contrary, belonged to the Church, the Army, and the respectable and law-abiding class of citizens. The obsessional European antagonism against the Jews now found an outlet in the writings of people of distinction. If they did not hate the Jews they certainly loathed the whole ideology which emanated from the newly articulate Jewry. Nietzsche spoke for many when he declared war on this 'morality of the weak', whose strength depended upon their success in popularizing peace as against war, the rights of the peaceful as against the violent warriors. Behind all this, in the villages particularly, the Judas bogy continued his spiritual reign.

Hitler's genius intuitively understood that the various

[1] Cf. esp. James Parkes, *Foundations of Judaism and Christianity*, 1960.

antagonisms could be united in the cry, and the implementation of the cry: 'Judah perish!' He identified the
members of the race Israel with the traditional bogy
and the theological enemy. By slaying Israel the whole,
real or imaginary, Jewish ideology would be killed. The
election of Israel would be shown as a deceitful charade
of weak profiteers, the God of Israel as the clownish
masque of a tribe of parasites. In the obscene pages of the
Stuermer as well as of scientific journals the dogma reached
its climax in the declaration of war on this vermin which
corrupted, infected, and de-humanized humanity and
whose extermination alone could save the world.

But this argument, if it can be called such, had the
effect that it removed the conflict from the purely
military sphere. This has been recognized in the courts,
where the plea of the defence (for example, by Servatius)
that there could be no question of personal guilt when
men merely obeyed military orders, was not upheld. The
judges, German and non-German, have held, on the
contrary, that although a military occupation provided
the opportunity for the extermination the crime was not
extenuated by this circumstance. The court reached the
verdict that genocide is a crime against humanity and
not an incident of war.

This judgment confirms our thesis that the problem
transcends that of a crime that can be measured in
physical terms. By fusing all existent resentments and
traditions connected with Anti-Semitism, Hitler introduced a spiritual factor. By his racial criterion not only
the Jews but also the Christian religion is thoroughly
condemned. For the first time, but too late, it dawned
upon the responsible Christian circles that Israel is not

only the cradle of Christianity, but that Jesus and the Apostles, being Jews, had bequeathed to the Christian tradition precepts irreconcilable with the new ecstatic faith of Nordic Superman. It may now seem unbelievable, but it is nevertheless true, that Christian Churches, and especially theologians, were enticed to such an extent that they saw only too late that Law, Prophecy, Wisdom, Gospel were rejected in common with the Jews.

The theological consequence of Auschwitz is therefore plain. We witness a physical conflict in which the legal, prophetic, and sapiential tradition of Israel clashes with the ideology of a totalitarian power. We have to interpret the physical defeat of the representatives of the former, the near-conquest of the world by the latter, the ultimate triumph of the remnant, and the eclipse of the dictator by the narrowest of margins.

Such an interpretation cannot be contained in economic, political, and military terms alone. The down-to-earth historical and biographical details, though always relevant, cannot satisfy our enquiry. At the same time we must not allow ourselves to be lured from the facts and indulge in the kind of quasi-mythology which the Nazis fancied. The Führer's demonic energy and the system's operation of an almost ritualistic pattern of humiliation and torment does not entitle us to adopt an otherworldly answer to our problem. A *Diabolus ex machina* is almost as bad and unhelpful as a *Deus ex machina*. Auschwitz was not a ritual drama. There was a system of extermination, but no solemnities in which a king visits the underworld, conquers death after mortal combat, and rises again victoriously to be acclaimed at the spring-tide as alive. Ancient paganism is conspicuous for its absence when we deal with electric wires and gas containers.

The problem of Auschwitz is theological in the fullest sense because it posits the ambiguity of human historical existence in a world created and sustained by God. Its meaning, or lack of it, cries out for transcendental reference. But transcendental terms, such as Providence for example, must be examined afresh in the light of the great catastrophe.

Such an interpretation must not take refuge in too many abstractions. The concrete reality, as given by history, must be compared and contrasted with the concrete reality of the divine self-disclosure. Thus a dialectic emerges in which the Cross of Christ interprets the tragic holocaust, and in which the contemporary scene reflects the eternal.

IV

THE ARREST

ALL ARRESTS ARE preceded by certain preliminaries. Christ anticipated even during his last meal with the disciples that one of them would betray him, leave under the protection of darkness, communicate with some in authority, and lead the soldiers to the secret place. There a kiss would serve as a token of recognition. A moment of hesitation follows, in which the possibility of resistance is encountered, only to be dropped immediately. The arms of man cannot defend the Son of Man, for he has chosen non-violence in order to bring his own work to perfection. The arrest is awful, and an atmosphere of terror touches even those who carry out the arrest. It seems inconceivable that perfect freedom should incontrovertibly hand itself over into the hands of men, to be taken and carried away. The climax of the arrest lies in the supreme paradox that freedom is vulnerable and that spiritual sovereignty is still liable to be arrested in conditions of time and space. Handcuffs, chains, ropes are the outward trimmings of the eclipse of divine freedom. The author of life is subjected to laws which ought to break at the sight of him, but the impersonal causes are stronger than the existential freedom of the Word and of Love. Hence, however much we may choose to mint phrases, the cold fact remains that Jesus at his arrest is prototype of all arrested against their essential nature of freedom.

Certain antecedents, however, help to explain the paradox. First of all, as a matter of strategy, Jesus went to Jerusalem, apparently intent upon this course of action which must be fraught with the danger of arrest. One may almost speak of a voluntary resignation. This voluntariness is buttressed by Jesus' strange attitude to life. He loved life and his ministry among men, but he did not consider 'normal' life to be the proper fulfilment of a human life. Marriage, the acquisition of property, the administration of an office, the institutionalized vocation, were altogether alien to his highly charismatic conception of the call from God. He could therefore in a sense easily envisage the termination of the normal life on earth, since he was inspired with the belief that an end to his own life must be a dramatic fulfilment. The arrest was therefore for him a necessity in an altogether predictable course of self-sacrifice. In him the 'must' of his destiny met the freedom of his royal and priestly vocation in a longing for a critical consummation of all things. Thus the New Testament surrounds his arrest not only with agony and fear, but also with sacrificial self-oblation. The arrest is a necessary stage in atoning sacrifice.

The theologian is, in fact, so used to the initiative in atonement, which the fourth Gospel attributes to Jesus himself, that at times the Passion narrative reads like the account of a charade. The human side is almost extinguished at the expense of a divine automaton who strides through the ordeal like a god whom nothing can touch. But the arrest demands a much greater theological subtlety than a charade can vouchsafe. The suffering alone during the long night of waking, the knowledge of the treachery, of sleeping and apparently indifferent disciples, the general air of misunderstanding on their part, excelled only by the meanness of the conspirators and the crude display of physical violence on the part of the soldiers, all these accessories to the arrest make it plausible to speak of the evil as one of impersonal darkness: 'For it was night'. Thus the New Testament pairs the inner guilt of all involved with an external givenness, as if Satan manipulated his puppets. The theological verdict follows that here God suffers an arrest by man; or, to be more precise, here the God-given Son runs to his eternal Father, bringing back to the Creator the tarnished creation, which at the moment of the arrest discloses its deadly opposition to the freedom of God and to the Spirit who bears the Son on his course of Sacrifice.

This theological framework, though uniquely couched in terms of Messianic self-giving, has done good service in accounting for individual martyrdom, Christian or otherwise. One can, for example, even think of Socrates as someone who welcomes his arrest, though he must denounce the injustice that has usurped his freedom. Similarly, the martyrs of our own time, such as Bonhoeffer, or, more latterly, in Africa, have not shrunk from the inevitable 'darkness at noon'. In as much as they jeopardized their lives and regarded them as stakes, by which they exposed their freedom to the restrictive cruelty of man, they could hardly complain when their hour also had come. Thus an Edith Stein, for example, though far from suicidal in intent, and preserving life for as long as possible by flight from Cologne to Echt, knew that the knock at the door for her, with the typically cruel 'Hurry up, you!', sealed a God-given freedom of the spirit. All these men and women echo the

'Suffering must be' (*Dei Pathein*) of their Lord in the moment of fearful finality. They know that by handing over their body their only remaining freedom lies in the obedience which turns the arrest into a voluntary dedication in sacrifice. Thus they achieve a theological interpretation by their intention and imitation of Christ.

But this interpretation founders when we survey the scene when a German SD detachment rounds up men, women, and children of a typical ghetto outside, say, Kiev or Riga. This is not so because the victims are Jews, but because they are human beings who, however miserable their conditions, existed like plants rooted in a poor soil. They were attached to it, for from it they got their living. The businesses they carried on, the little property they owned, the tradition they had inherited, could not prepare them for a heroic freedom in adversity. The nature of human society is to endow its group organism with normalcy, in which births and deaths occur as a matter of course. It is not its business to shoulder a deep destiny. The only 'must' of group existence is to ensure a continuity of life. It is not free to lead a prophetic life of freedom.

It is, therefore, impossible to find a rational or providential apology for the disaster which overtook these communities. The prophetic indictment, which we find in the Bible, does not apply to any modern community. The prophets arraigned the people of Israel for their unrighteous acts—murder, theft, adultery in particular—and their ungodly way of life and worship. They threatened them with sword, famine, pestilence, and death as the inevitable consequence of their hell-bent career. But the arrest of modern communities cannot be accounted for in these terms. First, it would be difficult to establish their guilt, as if in excess of other groups' immoralities; secondly, it would be idle to pretend that a modern community is free to respond to the prophetic ideal of moral perfection. At best one could say that some men and women, though no children, deserve their fate, always assuming that they were free to change their ways; but no one could wish to consign the whole to perdition because of its infection by the few.

The arrest of Christ makes sense in the terms of the whole Passion narrative; the arrest of our contemporaries makes no sense morally or spiritually, since they are torn away from their moorings, hurled together without discrimination and concession. Here individuals are broken down into an impersonal segment to be pounded into nothing. There is no freedom in this arrest, for the armed detachments and their unarmed victims are coerced by the system. Nevertheless, the enemy, who encircles, surrounds, shuts up, and cramps the faceless throng whom God has called to movement and freedom, evokes biblical memories: once again Jerusalem has fallen.

This, then, is not the arrest of Christ re-enacted. Instead of the amazing awe, which even the captors seem to have felt at Gethsemane, there is only brutal terror on the one hand, and trembling fear on the other. Where Christ can welcome the fulfilment of his self-willed destiny, our victims of the terror are wholly unprepared for their long journey into the dark. The continuity of Christ's work jars with the total ruin which they must suffer.

Yet it is in the darkness of the hour of arrest that a reflection of the light of Christ can be seen despite the wired fence and the towers manned by machine-guns. The arrivals are also innocent and unarmed. It is true, their lack of preparedness in most, though not all, cases has been cited as an accusation. In view of what happened it has been held that no men should ever find themselves unarmed. The question of 'the swords', first raised at Gethsemane, has acquired a new edge after Auschwitz. The defence of the civil population can certainly not be by-passed by a pious reference to Christ's arrest.

A defenceless multitude, who can neither fight nor hide nor escape, is not a theological ideal, but their plight places the victims within that long and honourable tradition of those who do no violence. Here interpretation can affect the picture in retrospect. Despite the heart-rending intensity of the cries of the innocent, who are barely conscious of what is going on, we may connect them with Rachel's children. It is our faith, then, which detects the ancient pattern of defeat, of the sheep before the shearer, the victim before the slaughter. These helpless people resemble the Servant of God, weak, poor, and less attractive than any man.

This tentative identification enables us to reconcile God's providence with the sufferings of Israel. The salvation of Israel cannot look to success in armed conflict, but must be found beyond the great endurance in a spiritual victory. Hence the arrest of the many fulfils, as did the self-oblation of Christ, the Servant prophecies: 'despised, rejected, struck with grief, smitten of God, afflicted, taken.'

Yet this identification must only intensify our quest for redemption. The anguish of the rounded-up on their way immediately evokes the picture of the Binding of Isaac, the so-called 'Aqueda'. The whole story of Genesis xxii with its dreadful economy of words reads like a Biblical commentary on the arrest. It terrified Kierkegaard about a century before Auschwitz occurred and he discerned there the incomprehensible predicament of man before God. Abraham's readiness to obey God's will on Mount Moriah seemed to him to fall outside the orbit of morality. God's command raises the radical question of faith. In heeding it we begin to grasp that the walk of father and son to the place of catastrophe is more than an enforced march, that a possibility remains after arrest and loss of freedom.

Nevertheless we cannot suppress the tragic discrepancy between story and event. In the former the father drops the knife, the lad is spared, and a substitute is found; in the latter there is no release to the spring of the trap of history. No remnant can run away from the sadistic enemy who issues his directives over the telephone across hundreds of miles.

There emerges, therefore, out of this arrest not only awe and wonder but a very rational theological responsibility for the innocent. It must articulate accusations, not only against the criminal authors of the arrest and society which allowed these events to take place, but against its own muffled voice. Such theological self-criticism is necessary lest Abraham's ordeal and the binding of Isaac be exploited to justify a mystique of necessary suffering. The identification of the type of suffering is not a subtle underwriting in theological irresponsibility.

This conscious defence of the innocents against false arrest is a precious legacy. It has often been muted through false pietism and cowardly appeasement. But if the arrest of the innocents recalls that of the children, who, according to the Gospel, were predestined to give their lives at the birth of Christ, it must, in the light of the path to Auschwitz, stimulate the theological protest against similar brutalities. Otherwise Biblical typology may well become an excuse for murder.

With this reservation we may attach the Christian parable to our history. Herod and the babes prefigure the round-up before the final solution. They impart a link to the drama of redemption. As the arrested stand outside their hovels, are lined up, counted, marched off, and squeezed into their temporary compounds, the far-distant innocent echo the transcendent possibility that this prelude to death may at length, in conjunction with Christ, stand within a spiritual pattern of eternal salvation beyond history.

Such a vista of hope was not granted to the arrested, except in those extraordinary cases where the few could transform their exile from the world into a meaningful oblation. Such a spiritual victory by faith is never granted by the historical condition but only by the Grace of God. It mediates the transcendent possibility where all other escape-routes are cut off. The letters from prison, which have survived, are the documentary evidence for this conquest; others were not even given the opportunity to write letters. A considerable body of witnesses demonstrates the limitation of totalitarian rule and the reality of the freedom of the spirit under arrest.[1]

[1] Cf. esp. Sergei Hackel, *One, of Great Price*, 1965, The Life of Mother Maria Skobtsova, Martyr of Ravensbrück, esp. chs. 8 and 9; E. H. Robertson, *Christians against Hitler*, 1962.

But this evidence cannot be rendered in propositional terms. It does not authorize the thesis that the arrest was a blessing in disguise or that good comes out of bad. It is more nearly related to the type of lamentation which we find in the Bible and in hymns of Church and Synagogue. In bewailing fate—theirs and ours—the lamentation casts infinite sorrow into prayerful form. It is an incantation against tyranny and sadism, a request for help against the unknown force which now enslaves men by machine-made and controlled cruelty.

A theology of Auschwitz cannot be written unless its findings issue in prayer, for we can face the horror only by coming to terms with it liturgically. Thus we are bidden to re-enact the arrest of the innocent. This prayer is an existentialist decision for the faith which links freedom with God. It releases in us the spirit which yearns to crown innocence with freedom. It articulates the need for an eternal reality of freedom and acknowledges God as the champion on the way to, and as the goal of, freedom.

V

THE TRIAL

THE PASSING FROM capricious despotism and mob rule to law is the epoch-making achievement of men of the second millenium before Christ. In Israel as elsewhere judgment depends upon custom administered by law-officers. Life is regulated in conformity with a covenant and the judges are the custodians of the right way. Their corruptibility is a constant theme in prophetic denunciations, but the prophets themselves are law preservers and not law-breakers. Indeed for them God's controversy with Israel is the one great indictment by which the people must stand or fall, for God maintains the right as he maintains life.

The picture of the assizes dominates world-history. The clash between right and wrong culminates in the trial when the accused faces the judge. The procedure safeguards the rights of the accused. The hearing is concerned with facts, not with rumour or personal grudges. The result of the trial is open until the verdict of guilty or the acquittal is pronounced. Sentence follows, and the death penalty covers serious cases of proven crime.

The ancient world knew its cases of the miscarriage of justice. Ahab at the instigation of Jezebel caused the death of Naboth and is denounced by Elijah as a royal murderer. Yet these cases are rare, and it may be remarked that only a very small number of prophets appear to have been executed for political sedition. Even Jeremiah escaped with his life. Similarly in classical Greece a case such as the unjust death sentence on Socrates by the State is the exception rather than the rule.

The existence of law enables even the unjustly condemned to use their trial as a demonstration for the right. The civilized procedure induces Socrates, for example, to stress and assess the guilt of his accusers and to meditate on his own share in their misguided fervour to annihilate him. He may even discuss the future, his own and theirs, and draw a moral lesson which will outlive the wrong judgment. He may go further still and view his death with ironic detachment and restrained piety and thus restore to the trial a sense of serene contentment.

The events following the arrest of Jesus do not fall into this category. The Gospels give an account of several trials which are difficult to assess. It seems that the conspirators behind the arrest were strangely taken aback by events. They appear to have forgotten that their activities would inconveniently collide with a high festival which must intervene and upset their plans. This is particularly strange considering that the conspirators appear to have been identical with those who were to try Jesus immediately after his arrest. A certain obscurity, then, surrounds the trial from the start. We cannot tell whether Jesus was in fact arrested during the night of the Passover and whether the prohibitions affecting the daily routine on that day impeded the course of the Jewish legal machinery. We cannot even tell with any certainty whether the enemies of Jesus meant such a legal machinery to operate, or whether they intended to set

aside the usual procedure in favour of a brazen disregard
for the forms of legality.

These uncertainties are not only of an historical
interest. They impede the striking of a moral balance-
sheet. The Gospels certainly appear to ascribe the guilt,
arising out of a deliberate violation of legality, to the
Jews. The priests and their minions aim from the start
at a death-sentence and therefore arrange a trial which is
wholly illegal. The people act as the mob which finally
yells for the prisoner's life. The Roman governor is by
comparison only weak and his soldiers are merely tools.

On the fatal day things must have looked different
from the portrayal handed down to us. In the Gospel
narrative decisions and actions are ascribed to whole
groups of people which cannot have decided and acted
with one voice. But despite this stylized report, which
reads like the direction for a staged performance where
'priests' and 'people' figure in unison, the tradition that a
highly irregular procedure was adopted cannot be gain-
said. There was a useless council after the arrest, another
trial on the morning of the following day which culminated in a condemnation without sentence. The hearing before Herod is unaccountable. The charges before
Pilate are wholly unrelated to what has gone before.

Furthermore the obscurity of the procedure also
imparts an enigmatic ambiguity to the charges brought
against Jesus. He is certainly accused of many things. He
has acted as a rebel, offended against the law (which
law?), determined to destroy the temple (and build it
again!); he claims to be the Messiah, the anti-king to
replace Caesar. He is both a political danger and a
blasphemer. Yet none of these charges are felt to be the

real point at issue. On the one hand Caiaphas expresses a quasi-mystical need for Jesus to die, and almost acts as a priest in the belief that the death of Jesus is a necessary ritual, whereas on a simpler level the majority of the priests are actuated by envy, i.e., an impatient instinct of self-preservation against claims which they hardly understand, except for their dislike of him who makes them. But this picture is furthermore confused by the sudden hostility of the mob (especially gathered and trained to shout for the release of Barabbas and the death of Jesus?) and the shadowy figures, such as Pilate and his assistants, Herod of Galilee (in Luke), Annas (in John).

The disorder of the narrative probably reflects an extraordinary course of action. It endows the killing of the Man with an historical penumbra of cold hatred, open cruelty, cynical illegality, mob fury, and moral cowardice. Lawlessness shows here its true face. Yet despite the yelling crowds, the beating soldiers, the smiling despot, the arguing priests, the silent witnesses, and the failing followers, everyone knows that the import of the trial and the movements from court to court is found elsewhere. The trial occurs, the movements cannot be stopped, the Jews and the Romans (which Jews, which Romans?) are involved in an action of which the whole world will know to their shame: yet none of these are more than assistants to him 'who suffered for us, leaving us an example'.

His trial is, in fact, his trial of the world. He acknowledges its debt and offers satisfaction for its debt; he knows its hostility and meets it in his person: as a lamb among tearing wolves, as a vindicator among the downtrodden, as a retribution for criminals condemned, as the expiation of the deep stain of sin, as the lover of the hating: as the redeemer of the forfeited race. The trials are the surface of the ordeal, a stage on which the accused transcends their course. The lawgiver, prophet, Messiah acts on behalf of the world, crowning his work by accusing the world which has brought him to trial.

The people destined for Auschwitz share with Jesus the immediacy of their destruction after their arrest. The camps were merely designed for transit. The people were kept on the move. There is an absence of legality from the start and the whole thing is part of a big scheme to end lawful civilization itself. It is the result of a conspiracy and the obscurity is part of the conspiracy. Dates and records disappear. Again the historical interest yields to a moral concern and focuses attention on the actors. The relationship between the leaders of the people, and of the people themselves, is difficult to define. The motivation is a blend of blind hatred, envy, and a quasi-mystical need to kill. Thus the ordeal of those about to die becomes a judgment by the condemned on their judges.

In this tremendous reversal of the roles the behaviour of the prisoner is of decisive importance. It is important to unmask the misrepresentation of the victims. When the blurred edges of civilization disappear naked self-interest is liable to take command in conditions of starvation and extreme privations. But the king rat, who establishes a corner in supplies and erects a hierarchy of lesser rats to administer the life and death of all under arrest, did not rule among those on trial before Auschwitz. In the transit camps this system of Antichrist had no time to develop. Moreover the moral character of the people countered the conditions with the unselfishness which alone could keep alive the weak, the sick, the very old and the very young. Despite the stunned state of the prisoners they performed notable deeds of humanity. The Spirit of God was not absent from the victims. It expressed itself in an endeavour to establish some kind of order, to provide water where there was none, milk for the children if at all possible, a fair distribution of food because of the grim scarcity, and the rudiments of sanitation.

The deportees' trial resembles, and differs from, that of Jesus. The confusion of the human scene during the transports approximates the chaos which affects the trials of Jesus. The anonymity of the guilty has the same haunting quality, though we know more about them than about the innocent. Their share in the crime— drivers, stokers, shunters, signalmen, clerks in offices— points to the guilt which is in the mind, now made manifest in the action.

Yet the deportees face no trial, not even the parody of a trial. They are collected for transport like animals for the slaughter. Whereas Jesus meets his enemies face to face in an encounter in which even the enemy receives some kind of stature, if only by hatred and envy, the deportees face no charges, except that of existence. They are not held responsible as human beings; they meet no accuser, no judge, no witnesses. Hence the deportees cannot share the grandeur of Christ in the hour of darkness. They cannot heroically profess their faith, like the martyrs.

They are now on trial against an enemy who is within. First, it is the body with its endless craving for food and drink. Physical existence becomes wholly degrading when its needs cannot be met. My body becomes then the index of my scope for suffering. It infects my mind with hopelessness or with a renewal of delusions. I imagine that all may be well in the end: 'they cannot behave like that; it must be an error. It is illegal. They will send us to Theresienstadt where things are said to be quite pleasant . . . etc.'

The physical instincts put the mind on trial in two particular ways. The desire for survival, whatever happens, at anyone's expense, even at the risk of betraying all, induces an immoral, clawing attitude. My neighbour becomes my enemy because he needs, like myself, air, food, drink, and space. Hence I am tempted to side with hell and all its devils if only I can live. On the other hand, I long to be quit of the torment and am tempted to universalize my desire for death in a feeling of total alienation.

The trial is, therefore, on its inner side not unlike the agony of Christ, especially since the deportees' sufferings concern not only themselves, but the fate of their children. Auschwitz is the huge fulfilment of Dostoevsky's vision of the godless world, which, in the words of Ivan Karamazov, merits only contempt, best conveyed by 'returning one's ticket', The children, as Dostoevsky notes, must not be taken as a sentimental veil, whereby we almost condone the crimes against adults. If no care be taken it could be argued that, since all the little ones will one day be big ones, we should not be too nice about children. But the torment of the children is of its own kind. It has a long history in the denial of God and man. The Assyrians appear to have ripped the babes from their mothers' womb and killed infants. The camp officers have had children starved, clubbed to death, strung up, burned alive, machine-gunned, and gassed. We take this to be the totalitarian equivalent to the spitting at, and the beating of, the Son of Man.

At this stage of the trial we are no longer concerned with the offence against the law. The Ecce Homo before Pilate brings to a fine point the dignity of Man and the unspeakable horror of sin. The children at Auschwitz similarly convict us of an undefinable darkness, to which words like 'trespass' or 'rebellion' simply cannot give expression. The evil is of such dimensions that it discloses an even unsuspected degree of guilt in the whole human race, and it is this knowledge of evil which cries out for an atonement which no man can work.

Through this identification the sufferings of the tried are saved from meaninglessness. Its spiritual value is established and proves inexhaustible. It cannot be brushed aside by other, better experiences. It cannot be disposed of in any way. The cause of the children of Auschwitz is the cause of God himself among men. Thus, though some would cite the evidence of the children as proving incontrovertibly the existence of a world without God, the Spirit of God defies in us the atheistic conclusion of absolute despair. He discloses himself again as the God of the slaves in the brick-kilns of Egypt, as the father of the children who leads them through desert and flood, Exile and Babylon, on the painful road to the humanization of mankind. The *via dolorosa* of the railway is the *via dolorosa* of God.

The modern stations of the Cross are unlit and the procession leads to an Auschwitz from which there is no return. They evoke a standing still in contrition, a contemplative gaze, and a dirge of pity. But the voices from the final station admonish: 'Weep not for us, weep for yourselves!'

VI

ARRIVAL

THE INMOST DESIRE of men is to arrive at their des-
tination. We come and go, but the meaning of all movement is to place at length the object where it belongs, or
to settle ourselves in, what we call, home. This home-
coming is rightly associated with the course of our life.
We go forth from the unknown, we are born, we traverse
the rough and smooth passages of middle life, and wisdom
is our guide to welcome the light in the window of death.
Caressed to the end, nursed and loved, and ultimately
in a state of felicitious unconsciousness, with friendly
salutations to bid us farewell, and with spiritual en-
couragement to speed us on our journey, we are
ready to take our departure. For to depart is to
arrive.

Not so at Golgotha, nor at Auschwitz. The account
of Jesus's arrival at the place of the skull, scourged,
bruised, mocked, and faint, excels in matter-of-fact
brevity. One Simon carried the cross-beam of the Cross,
the upright stake being already in position. Whether the
women succeeded in offering refreshment to Jesus or not
is open to question. Certainly he remains wholly conscious as he reaches the spot of execution which we can
no longer fix with any certainty. The soldiers are ready
for him; the victim is stripped naked. Nails or thongs
were used to fasten his body to the cross-beam on the

ground, which was then fixed to the upright stake. Then the feet were also fastened, and the man on the cross had to wait for death through exhaustion. Now for Jesus the body is also the seat of shame. Rigid and immobile, exposed to the public gaze, tortured by hunger, thirst, and insects, he hangs. He has arrived. Two criminals suffer near him. His loved ones approach. Helplessness and darkness, not a helping hand and soft comforts, mark the arrival of the servant of God.

Now it is the human condition itself, and not detailed facts nor specific culprits, which must be arraigned before God. The indictment against this monstrous state cannot be softened by theological overtones, such as that all men must die, and that it pertains to a life of sacrifice to be given. Here is the hard core of cruelty, symbolized by parched lips and burning flesh, which seeks expiation. The Cross is here not symbol of salvation, but of horror, the age-old horror of the arrival at despair which no words can alleviate. 'Did heaven look on, and would not take their part?'

The moment of arrival holds in itself the terror of what has been, of what is, and of what must come. Every joy of the past, every smile and laughter, all exchanges of love, recede as the trucks open to unload their human content, staggering from amidst the fouled floor on which the dead lie still and the dying writhe. Among the children some still clutch a toy in death. The guards inspect, shout, threaten, beat. The slow and the crippled are knocked down, the sick and the aged must be encouraged to speed up. For there is no time to lose at this platform of arrival, the station of Auschwitz where the train has stopped. Here is the famous fence, the wooden, somewhat old-fashioned crenellated battlement, with its greeting, promising that work makes for freedom.

Thick forests, piled up snow and an empty plain mark the place of arrival. Searchlights, lorries, voices—it is a world, real yet dream-like, a nightmare without any apocalyptic signs. Order prevails. Which order? A dividing up of the wretched togetherness which even the camp had not yet broken up before. Husbands, wives, children, luggage dissolve into fragments. Most go up the ramp, past the doctor, who decides over life and death. Arrival there and passing him means death.

Oh, welcome death! The cross bears the body which burns, the overfilled huts hold bunks which, if they were like beds, would give way under the weight of endless bodies. Within the extermination-camp thousands file through. A few nights and days, and the arrivals press upon the former arrivals, providing an endless stream which only death can contain. We arrive to wait for the end.

Woe to the lucky ones, whose arrival summons new hopes, because they are privileged to be driven to the rubber works where prison labour is to complete a synthetic plant, which was never to yield a pound of rubber. Woe to the thousands, of whom one may survive! The thirst for life postpones their departure, does not save them. Here the Cross is elongated in time, by days, weeks, months.

To be selected to labour service after arrival is to be face to face with the human condition which, under diabolical direction, is entirely devised to crush humanity. To arrive for death, and then for death to be kept at arm's length, so as to squeeze the last ounce out of the imprisoned human condition, is a torture which Jesus could not know. Now to be stripped naked, to have one's hair cut, to be registered, tattooed, marked, dressed in thin cotton, ready for a roll-call, shivering on the parade ground, and—the worst irony—always compelled to co-operate in order to 'survive', i.e., to obey that cursed instinct despite a complete lack of hope—this is the final humiliation of the arrival in hell. To avoid the floggings and hangings, to join the ranks of the organizers, pimps, criminals, to find something to offer for sale in abject poverty, not to be submerged in the flood of suffering, to flatter the king rat, to stand well in his calculating scheme: why does man endure it? Because although he would say a thousand times that he would rather cough away his last breath at arrival, he cannot help breathing in. He has, physically and spiritually, a longing to breathe in and out, to eat, to drink, to love, to see 'another butterfly', to 'go home again and live', as the children put it when waiting at Theresienstadt.

This human condition overwhelms all men. The Lord's 'I thirst' reproduces the cry of anguish which thousands uttered on lifting heavy weights, and, above all, dragging their emaciated bodies on sore feet against which the ill-fitting clogs rubbed until the fever set in and terminated labour and life. This 'I thirst' immediately induces the parallel cry of despair: 'My God, why hast thou forsaken me?'

This physical and spiritual cry has with Jesus the subtle overtone of quotation. By articulating words familiar from the Psalms he sets his suffering against the framework of known personal piety and cultic order. But the human condition in its immediacy of suffering normally excludes the art of quotation. The exhaustion of the aching body and the blood-starved brain mocks all existentialist confidence. Existence is simply pain and loneliness. All ways to an escape are barred. Formerly acquired knowledge proves useless. Memories add sorrow to pain. Spiritual insights of the past are blotted out. Hence the thirst is as self-defeating as the momentous quest after God.

The transcending of this human condition must be miraculous. Jesus achieved it, some men at Auschwitz also testify to the survival of the human spirit through the all-transcending Grace in the total absence of the means of Grace. The miracle is performed by the forsaken and amongst the wholly unexpected. It has nothing to do with education or physical resilience. The successful organizers may achieve survival, but they ruin their souls. They prolong life at the expense of the human spirit. The poison of the system acts upon them as an antibiotic which, by reducing life to the meaningless, keeps the biological function going somewhat longer. But the forsaken look for more than the prolongation of life. Jesus lived for three hours on the cross and did not descend from the cross nor feign death.

The miracle depends upon sovereign Grace acting upon the spiritual will. The forsaken answers his own cry with the tragic realization that the legions of angels do not come to his assistance. Silence reigns. 'Why do you not come to heal my wounds?', 'Why do you not break through the clouds and restore me?' repeats the anxious soul, until there dawns the greater realization: MY GOD, I COME TO THEE. The arrival is a home-coming after all through the release of such a vision of life, a vista of a future so amazing, that the earthly arrival platform is already seen in its true colours. Sun, moon, and stars are now the witnesses to a new theme: the personalization of the world in God.[1] The obedience to the human condition is also the departure from the human condition, the break-through from existence to essence. The pain, the thirst, the despair are the paving stones to the bridge to eternity. God of darkness, God of light; God of suffering, God of comfort; God absent, God present—the Father discloses his being in the quarry, under the sacks of coal, under the weight of the sleepers, in the washing and gassing chambers, erected by Topf & Söhne, Erfurt. But the miracle is rare, and the vision is of Grace where Hell reigns.

The peril of theological speculation is to speak too soon, too confidently, as if to cash in on the unknowable experience of Grace. There is no doubt that for some the climax to suffering is not the dreaded deadlock, but the heroic act of self-transcendence, the entry into the divine harmony, not by an illusory mirage born out of a feverish delirium, but an inward conviction. The theological confidence, however, is soon shaken by the fact that only the few and elect can pass thus from the extreme negation to the infinite affirmation. This passage is best illustrated by the head crowned with thorns and the body pitted with spikes, the mouth open with flowing saliva and the skin green with incipient putrefaction— as shown in Grünewald's famous Isenheim altar piece —and the highly stylized, royal and self-possessed Lord

[1] Teilhard de Chardin writes of his vocation: 'Personnaliser le Monde en Dieu' as part of his tremendous conception of a cosmic and loving universe. (*Lettres de voyage*, p. 200.)

whom Raphael and his school portray in many versions. The aesthetic gulf between the two speaks of the tension between the IT of the hanging and the HIM who has arrived at the end of his pilgrimage in fidelity. The wood of the tree signals the presence of a cosmic paradox: a mechanism of meaningless death and a life-giving dominion.[1]

Both at Golgotha and at Auschwitz this tension leads to a resumption of relationships. The Lord unites his mother and his disciple in a bond of mutual love. He enjoined both to take their place in his love. A new creative freedom issues from the depth of hell. Even the pleading criminal does not ask in vain for assurance and from cross to cross echoes the promise of Paradise. The Lord gives being to the people around him: Be a mother, be a son, be with me. Of love it was said in the ecstasy of loving that it was stronger than death. Now, shorn of all movement and denied all ecstasy, with the flesh in decay, the spirit mightily triumphs and announces the indestructibility of love. Even at Auschwitz this spirit prevails. Primo Levi writes objectively, certainly not as a mystic, when he greets Lorenzo as a man, a human being, pure, immaculate, beyond the world of negation, imparting miraculous humanity through constant care and being present. The redemptive divinity of cosmic dimensions reaches man by humanity.

The remission of sins from the Cross constitutes the apex of this redemptive activity. Jesus' prayer 'Father, forgive them, for they know not what they do' shatters the

---

[1] Cf. Augustine's famous summary: 'The tree upon which were fixed the limbs of Him dying was ever the chair of the Master teaching.'

bounds of likes and dislikes, rights and wrongs, appearances and reality. It becomes later a typically Christian ideal. The first martyr Stephen and countless others, after him and to this day, pray the prayer of forgiveness in order to achieve the mighty resolution to forgive. Thus the prayer becomes an *act* of forgiveness. It sanctions a change of relationship where love conquers hatred by the break-up of the solidity of hatred itself. Thus a mastery over evil can by one word proclaim a new era of new men.

At Auschwitz the freedom of this word cannot be heard and cannot be expected to be heard. The word 'forgiveness' becomes meaningless in many settings which the modern world provides. If I am to forgive someone I need at the same time the authority to make my pardon meaningful. If I have no power of reprieve I cannot meaningfully pardon. Now if my enemies are unknown to me, as when I suffer from criminal officialdom, I can hardly be expected to seek the conciliation of an anonymous and ever-changing institution. All serious exculpations demand the existence of a relationship between men known to one another.

But semantic misgivings only touch on the fringe of the problem. Forgiveness is a concept which governs a whole world of vital feelings. Auschwitz certainly stands in the tradition of the Cross that it also raises the issue of forgiveness. A neutral settling of the account is out of the question. These deeds cry out for revenge or for forgiveness. The grapes have been trodden, the red juice flows, the harvest of a moral evaluation cannot be kept at bay.

Yet the legacy of Auschwitz simply cannot be avenged. It cannot be reduced to the tremendous romance of a

Moby Dick whom Captain Ahab seeks out for a final duel in which the mighty white whale must perish together with the avenger and his crew. We cannot kill that which killed in order to arrive at moral restitution, any more than we can achieve the right by forgetting the wrong.

The prayer which Jesus utters to the Father is not an act of condonation nor an attempt at oblivion. It is an intercession on behalf of men whom he had either known personally or by repute, or whom the chance of the procedure had thrown in his way. Their 'ignorance' is not a lack of theoretical insight, nor the not-knowing which the Greek philosophers believed to be responsible for evil acts. Rather Jesus surveys the inner character of all participants in the passion, from Judas to Caiaphas, from Pilate to the centurion, and like Hosea and the prophets sees into their heart: 'They do not know'. Their lack of knowledge is a total blindness to the divine in creation, in election and covenant, in human relationships. They are not 'my people' and therefore bereft of mercy. They are themselves excluded from God, be they Israelites or pagans. But their personal guilt is even here seen to connect with their public role, which, as Caiaphas seems to have known according to the Fourth Gospel, lies within the providence of God. It is, therefore, an act of the overflowing Grace to acquit them and even to absolve them from the personal share in the public guilt and to open up before them the vista of the new age. The prayer for forgiveness challenges all to repent and to see with their eyes, to hear with their ears, to open their hearts to a return to God. It does not abrogate the moral calculus, does not absolve the hardened criminal, exonerate the deeds which have been committed. It raises the whole event to a timeless predicament, to a choice after all choices seemed to have been made. It avenges the impersonal past by holding out personal responsibility in a spiritual future.

All Christian acts and interpretations of martyrdom have followed this pattern. Yet at Auschwitz it would seem to break down, not only because the victims were for the most part not Christians nor willing martyrs. Rather, the nature of the guilt makes it extremely questionable whether even this interpretation of forgiveness can still be morally upheld. We are in the extraordinary position that our moral feelings tend to be outraged even by talk of forgiveness in this connection. The German Government has rightly insisted that it can make restitution as far as is possible, but it has never hinted that the financial payments can 'make good' the outrage which has been committed in the name of the German people. At the same time, the Government of Israel has also rightly insisted that the children cannot for ever incur the stigma of the guilt of the parents.

But such movements of restitution and conciliation, desirable as they are, hardly touch the legal conception of retribution and have nothing to do with the spiritual realm of atonement.

No one has anticipated the heart of our problem as Dostoevsky in *The Brothers Karamazov*. Again it is Ivan who analyses it with lacerating clarity, and it will suffice to follow him: he begins by his penetrating thought that the whole problem of the love of man and God is involved in the problem of guilt and retribution. 'Christ-like love for men is a miracle impossible on earth'; we

are not gods. For us suffering is our own. There are
degrees of suffering, and each one excludes the other and
alienates men. Suffering is not on the stage: it is real, not
in silk and lace. But the field is so enormous that it is
better to reduce the argument to the sufferings of the
children, who have not yet had time to 'eat of the apple'
and to become 'like gods'. Next Ivan describes in detail
the very atrocities committed against the children (and of
which Auschwitz is now our measuring rod). In passing
he notes that capital punishment is no answer to the
moral problem of murder; how much less is there an
answer to the torturing of children. 'It is their defenceless-
ness that tempts the tormentor, that sets his vile blood on
fire.' At Auschwitz there were examples of this, although
on the whole routine, dispassionate killing was the order
of the day. The tearing to shreds of the naked boy by the
hunting hounds, set on him, by the mad general, is for
Ivan the climax: what did he deserve? To be shot? 'To be
shot for the satisfaction of our moral feelings?'

The rest of the argument can be summarized coldly:
If there is an impersonal law of cause and effect, then no
one is guilty. Murderer and murdered are but victims of
their circumstances. If there is justice it demands a
vindication which is inconceivable. Revenge does not
restore life; recompense in the life after death is too
uncertain. If suffering is necessary for eternal harmony,
the evolution of the best of all possible worlds, then the
price is too heavy because it is immoral. Solidarity of
sin explains nothing. What then is to be done? Is a
celestial amnesty the answer in which the heroic share,
by forgiving too?

Ivan plays with the idea: 'When the mother embraces

the fiend who threw her child to the dogs, and all three cry aloud with tears: "Thou art just, O Lord!", then, of course, the crown of knowledge will be reached and all will be made clear. But what pulls me up here is that I can't accept that harmony.' Why not? Are we not sinners too, standing in need of forgiveness? Can we not enter the common pool of benevolence and 'forgive them, as he forgives us?' Ivan judges that 'it is not worth it'; a harmony bought at such a price can be no harmony. Ivan sees equally clearly that the conception of hell is of no help here, just as we know that an eternal Auschwitz provides no moral or emotional satisfaction to any reasonable man. But Ivan reaches what must be the fine point of the terrible reality: The mother cannot embrace the tormentor. 'She dare not forgive him!' Even if the child were to forgive him, she dare not. And so he concludes that he would rather be left with unavenged suffering and unsatisfied indignation.

This reasoning leaves out of account the place of penitence in forgiveness, and in most 'ordinary' cases of wrong one debt cancels out against another through the common pool of repentance. Such an act of repentance presupposes that the wrong can be undone by a renewal of the heart on the side of the penitent who, though he cannot undo the harm, can profess a genuine intention of doing reparation. This way of making spiritual reparation is the normally accepted application of Christian forgiveness.

Few of the war criminals have been found to show any signs of repentance and it is inconceivable that atonement can be made out of their tears. If they had, like the very few (e.g., Frank, the governor of Poland during the occupation), the problem would perhaps for some, if not for all, be open to the kind of reconciliation which Ivan rejects. It could then be argued, not coldly but with the reason of the heart, that the infinite merits of Christ attract to themselves the most grievous sins so that forgiveness may result. The call to self-transcendence implies a release from the scales of worldly justice, and justification by faith validates the possibility of such a conciliation. Perhaps the 'treasury of merit' includes the prayers of such saints as suffered at Auschwitz without any longing for revenge. Thus we know that the inter-cessions of Edith Stein have come to the aid of SS men after the war.

The Church has throughout the ages endeavoured to mitigate the harshness of condemnation. She has modi-fied the extreme view that there is only one forgiveness of sins, i.e. at Baptism. She has resisted the rigorist view that those who 'sin for a second time' cannot be saved. 'Though the great gate of forgiveness has been barred and bolted at baptism' writes Tertullian (during his orthodox days), 'second penance waits in the vestibule to open a postern door once more to those who knock'. He offers a 'plank in the shipwreck' and stimulates a long line of moralists who restrict damnation, seeing that reconcilia-tion is the aim of the Gospel.[1] This attitude goes much further than making over credit balances from the surplus of the saints to wipe out the penitent sinners' deficiency.

But the Church's dealing with sin among the faithful cannot be the same thing as our assessment of the guilt of Auschwitz. The former is continually oscillating, as it must, between a strict condemnation of anti-Christ,

[1] Cf. K. Kirk, *The Vision of God*, 1931, passim, esp. pp. 222 ff.

Satan, Sin, all of which are conceived as operating in enticing the faithful to evil deeds, particularly to the recanting of the faith and the degradation of apostasy; and, on the other hand, a liberalizing discipline which recognizes, especially during the passing of the ages, that man is a fallible creature and that he must be trained to become as perfect as possible. The often-despised veneer of Christian civilization at least produced the possibility of an ascetic, a reformatory and educational conception, in which both suffering and forgiveness occupy a perfectly acceptable place. Thus even mortal sin, when repented of on a deathbed, can be expiated by the will in the confession of sins.

The inapplicability of this improving and civilizing doctrine of the atonement, in which the propitiation of hostile powers is carefully balanced with the example of Christ's life—thus blending a transcendental and mystical conception with a practical outlook—becomes only too self-evident at Auschwitz. Ivan Karamazov had to reject the doctrine in view of what he had seen. Arguing from the particular to the general, he concluded that such a metaphysic jumped too many fences. It is true that Dostoevsky sees to it that this rigorism perishes with Ivan,[1] who knows quite well that one cannot live with the unavenged resentment rankling bitterly in the blood, and makes Alyosha, his saintly brother, overcome the world of hatred by conciliating the wronged child. But even so, the happy ending, with the children and Alyosha blending their voice in happy praise, is good stuff for a novel. Will it pass the gates of Auschwitz?

[1] I assume that D., had he continued the saga, would not have saved Ivan from the consequences of his brain-fever.

I do not myself believe that there can be forgiveness for Auschwitz, and I do not think that the words of Christ apply here. Not only the monstrosity, but also the impersonal 'nothingness' of the evil render this remission immoral and impossible. There is a sin against Man and Spirit which Christ declared to be unforgivable, and Auschwitz is this sin against Man and Spirit. It is the supreme act of blasphemy, and the men and tools who caused it neither desire nor can receive the forgiveness of their sin.

The Biblical refrain 'Vengeance belongs to God' in answer to the impasse rids man—and theology—of a more precise statement on matters of retribution. It hardly acts as a deterrent against further misdeeds of the ever-active potential of the imitators of Auschwitz. The daubs on synagogues and graves, not to mention more serious racial murders, are a present reminder that we are not talking about past history when we welcome a deterrent, even if it be called by the old-fashioned name Hell. But, unfortunately, Auschwitz itself has shown that as a practical deterrent the concept of the vengeance of God is not effective, for it is precisely the tormentors of mankind who ignore its prospects and laugh it off with a shrug of the shoulder and a shot from the pistol.

Thus the behaviour of the guards at Auschwitz and the very system of dehumanization with which we are concerned compels a more serious attitude to the whole concept of retributive justice. The classical age of a stylized Hell is no longer with us, where even the horrors of the abyss could be included in the 'Comedy'. But as the SS doctor Kremer rightly remarked: 'Dante's Inferno seems almost a comedy', in comparison with the realities of the extermination camp. Perhaps the SS doctor was not an expert in Dante studies, for even the medieval concept of the circles of hell, under a hierarchy of patron tormentors, both inspires terror and is written as a moral deterrent. The evil powers in hell hold each other in the grip of constant envy and hatred. Sartre's analysis of 'my neighbour, my enemy' on earth corresponds to that final picture of a mutual devouring by those engulfed in slimy cold filth.

Ignoring the mythological overtones of this picture, however, its central teaching also runs into trouble after Auschwitz. It is seen to eternalize the state of affairs which defies the laws of humanity. It seems barely conceivable that God should decree an eternal Auschwitz so that, by way of reciprocation, the sins of Auschwitz be satisfied. This would take the doctrine of vindication to an extreme metaphysic of reversal, and thus saddle the Kingdom of God with a counterpart, the Satanic realm. Symmetry prevails in this case over the alleged sovereignty of the good and loving God.

The inadequacy of the stark alternatives, Heaven and Hell, has been mitigated in the past by the creation of Purgatory, where the middle souls, for which the either-or of Heaven and Hell makes no provision, may continue their upward ascent of cleansing. Strictly speaking, these are the souls of those whose sins are forgiven, but whose recompense of wrong-doing is lacking. Their lack leaves a stain which needs to be burnt away. It is not material to our argument that Protestants have steadfastly refused to accept this compromise, mainly on the grounds that it created the abuses, such as indulgences and prayers for the dead, which the Reformation sought to abolish. Far more material is the realization that the world of Auschwitz simply does not move in a world of gradual ascent, of souls being made perfect by processes analogous to the refinement of precious metals. The evil-doers of Auschwitz are as hard as steel and as dark as pitch. Their cynicism does not accord with the stages of spiritual illumination, whether in this life or in the next.

The whole character of Auschwitz is at odds with Dante's and Milton's conception of the underworld. Dante's condemned men correspond to the mortal sins which they have committed. They show even in Hell a certain grandeur. The rebel is still a person to be reckoned with. Even the unpalatable doctrine of the saints' enjoyment in watching the torments of the damned, which St. Thomas Aquinas saves from being wholly disreputable, is not entirely incomprehensible in such a setting. To see Odysseus and Brutus and a wicked Pope confronted with the eternal reality and to suffer from the truth in Hell is to the poetical imagination a theme too mighty to be dismissed.

Morally speaking, however, this eschatology fails on a number of decisive considerations, when we put Hitler, Himmler, Hoess and their companions in their respective bowges. Even the saints would not want to see them. Their recognition of the truth is unthinkable, and their torments, far from yielding satisfaction, invalidate the whole of the Christian vision of eternal life. Even the admission that we carry within us the germs of their hell —'*simul justus simul peccator*' is the cliché of this important insight—cannot serve as an excuse to perpetuate a state of near-psychosis. The recognition of some psychologists (e.g. C. G. Jung) that our shadows are powerful, and represent to some extent the diabolical fantasies which others actually carry into practice, is in fact a powerful theological deterrent against a conception of hell which would eternally feed on this madness.

The contribution to the doctrine of hell is therefore a clear-cut refusal to grant perpetuity to horror and nothingness. It is an inducement to take seriously the realization that life without God is nothingness and that the abolition of man is precisely the earthly experience of a nothingness which has no right of survival. In short, what the Bible calls Death is the only possible equivalent to the minders of the death-machine. Extirpation is congruous with the feverish activists in annihilation. Damnation is the silent seal on their wickedness. Unforgiven and unforgivable they go to the doom which their own fantasies and crimes have already sought on earth. The apocalyptic torment which they administered is not for them. They are self-condemned in the nothing which they are. Their mean and cruel banality attains to the frustration inherent in nothing.

Yet it may be felt that this consequence of self-condemnation does not amount to a vindication of the cause of the oppressed. It was certainly felt to be so in the scholastic discussion of the problem. St. Thomas, for example, reasonably concludes that seeing the wickedness of the reprobate it is unthinkable that they would administer to themselves any punishment. Since they admit no pangs of conscience they must be made to suffer *ab extra*, i.e., against their own will which obviously would reject anything contrary to their own desires. But Auschwitz puts an end to such a moral necessity, for if our analysis of its nothingness is anywhere near the truth no further measures are necessary for the punishment of its perpetrators. They are their own executioners, and the vindication of the righteous and of the righteous cause occurs on a higher plane than the exposure of their nothingness.

We seem to have travelled a long way from the ramp where the arrival had to become the place of departure, where curses and despair drowned the voice of forgiveness and the remission of sins. But only in travelling thus far, over the ancient realms of retribution could we recover that light of freedom and rekindle that hope which sets the children free from their tormentors. We have at length reached the right to forget them. Not for them are the strains of the *Requiem aeternam*, not for them the absolution from sin and the enjoyment of bliss. Theirs is no mystery of transformation. As the wires still hang aimlessly in the air and as the tracks are overgrown which lead through the ridiculous battlement to the long platforms where no more trains arrive to unload children from trucks, so they who caused the misery recede like ghosts into the cold air. The dark night of the day of wrath remains for them. No judgment is given, no trumpet sounds, no summons is issued, no books are opened. The chant to the king of tremendous majesty for pity, for salvation, cannot be sung for them. No archangel descends to collect their souls in the world-wide offering of sacrifice and homage. In the darkness the shades blend with the blackness until complete indifference engulfs them.

May they never arise again!

VII

END AND BEGINNING

JESUS DIED ON the Cross after no more than three hours.
He was about thirty years old and his death occurred
somewhere around the year A.D. 30. The Gospel tradition suggests that death occurred earlier than could
normally be expected. The two fellow victims evidently
had to endure a longer ordeal. But we have no evidence
as to the circumstances of the death of Jesus, whether,
for example, he died 'voluntarily', as it is said of some
Africans that they have the power of 'voluntary dying'.
It is enough to know the unequivocal fact that Jesus died
like any human being, probably from shock and
haemorrhage.

Before his death he committed himself to the Father in
the words of Psalm xxxi, verse 5: 'Into thy hand I
commit my spirit', leaving it to the bystanders to complete: 'for thou hast redeemed me, o God of truth.' His
last moments were given to a survey of his short life and
he gave the verdict on his own suffering, thus completing
the self-transcending, freedom-establishing work, which
he had begun during his trial and effected throughout the
three hours of dying. The enemy no longer had any
power over him if death itself could be integrated into the
pattern of redemption. Could the inevitable process of
dying, the annihilation of self by the removal of body,
name, and memory, be overcome, as the world had been

overcome by forgiveness and judgment, by intercession and love? Could the true God still be seen as the omnipotent and blessed Father after his Son had tasted the bitterness of defeat? The one Greek word 'Tetelestai'— It is completed!—enforces the final Credo, a cosmic assertion that the Word does not return void in itself, to a void, and for nought. The victim contradicts the open spectacle which he, naked and already putrefying at his wounds on which the flies settle, gives to the world. He is his own evidence against the evident sight of the victory of the chaos. He sustains, though dying, the belief in a reality of goodness and love in the Divine Being.

This victory cannot be stated in merely human terms. Jesus, like other men, though few, may have hoped that his work will be perpetuated (though he wrote nothing down), that his band of disciples will be to him what children are to parents; but in other respects he had less to hand on than the rich and the mighty. There is no form of government, no artistic tradition, not even a bit of property and a settled estate. The obscurity of his life does not help us to interpret his death as the end of the old, and the beginning of the new, age.

But end and beginning can be altogether misleading terms of interpretation. To look at his imminent death and to sigh with relief that the torment is over, that he has tasted the suffering to the dregs of the cup of terror, that, in short, the chapter of the human tragic condition is closed by death: such a view misses both the paradox and the never-ending glory of the cross. The New Testament, without which we could know nothing of Jesus and his last moments, interprets his death not only as an example of pious dying, an act of resignation to be followed by all who are in the same predicament. This man certainly dies like other men, but he transforms through his dying the meaning of suffering and the destiny which we call death.

The moment of death is accordingly the climax of what we call the purpose of life, not its defeat or even its interruption. He and God are inseparable in death, in as much as he hands himself wholly to the Father, and the Father receives the dying Son in the eternal relationship of Love. Jesus had become the outcast of men in order to attain to this consummation. This man had taken upon himself this humiliation and submission to an agonizing death in order to free those who have no escape from the common pit.

Thus Jesus completed an eternal work upon the cross according to the Gospel message. The murder and the execution were the last stages in the manifestation of transcendent glory. As the Word glorified God in the Creation so in the act of redemption the same eternal Glory was displayed. The fulfilment of the Scripture was not a grammatical exercise, but a cosmic operation in which the Spirit sealed the transitory with the stamp of eternity.

Death as fulfilment is the paradox which Christ authorizes and which the dead of Auschwitz articulate. The contradiction stems not from historical chance, but from the divine purpose itself. Christ the eternal Word becomes flesh in time and space; Christ the Wisdom is manifested as folly among the wise; Christ the Power stumbles in weakness; Christ the Glory is seen as shame. Thus the death of Christ is the divine attestation for a truth which human reckoning of evidence does not

acknowledge. It is the decisive authority for looking at
the dying at Auschwitz beyond the man-given terms of
murder.

Auschwitz occurred in a century wholly estranged
from this paradox. It began with ideals of progress
altogether alien to a belief in one 'who died according to
the scriptures for our sins'. A positive evaluation of death
had vanished as the secular hope grew, and Jews and
Gentiles sang 'Brothers to freedom, brothers to the sun!'
Revolutionary martyrdom was politically exploited and
stood outside the framework of making reparation for
sin by atonement. After the First World War, when
death had been found chancy and meaningless, traditional feelings and statement about 'immortal sacrifice'
came to be regarded with increasing cynicism. Seen in
the light of the indiscriminate slaughter a wave of bitterness sprang up which regarded even Christ's crucifixion
as all sorts of things, mainly political, rather than the
life-giving death which the New Testament proclaimed.
Among the thoughtful the search for a meaningful life
continued in directions opposed to atonement. A meaningful death becomes the property of individuals. 'Die
your own death,' writes Rilke, in language reminiscent
of the Christian desire but averse to the cross. The saving
reality is now the integrity of each person and in that
sense I am my own saviour and my death crowns my
individuality. There is no enemy, there are no demons, as
long as I can come to terms with my own fantasies.

The holocaust of Auschwitz seems, however, stub-
bornly inexplicable in terms of the well-worn thought-
forms of a non-sacrificial background. Even the sacrificial
terms 'holocaust', or the Hebrew 'Churban', are used

superficially because the paradox has been overlaid with non-sacrificial theories.

This mass extermination really was a holocaust and was known to be such. The children outside the camps in Germany used to speak of 'going up through the chimney' as they had formerly done of terrors such as the bogey man. Similarly the prisoners knew that there was no way out of Auschwitz except 'by the chimney'. Only some of the new arrivals who were taken straight to their deaths may have been unaware of the process. Men and women were separated, made to strip naked so as to prepare for a bath as if in the interest of hygiene, escorted to the gas chambers which were immediately adjacent. Into these chambers the victims were pressed until there was no capacity for any more. They were pressed so tight that no one could fall down even at the moment of death. The guards have left notes of their impression of the actual gassing by cyclon B. As might be expected, some victims died sooner than others; from five minutes to twenty minutes the agony may have lasted. Some tried to fight their way out and wounded their immediate neighbours; others submitted with dignity and calm to their inevitable doom. It can be said from the evidence given by their executioners that death reigned here in every hue among the millions who suffered the same fate. When the chamber was re-opened special detachments of prisoners were responsible for the removal of the corpses to the crematoria. After the extraction of the gold from teeth, and such hair and skin as might prove useful, the fire left only a mass of ashes, which in their turn were used as agricultural fertilizers. The men who acted in these last transports were duly gassed and burnt after a short time and their place taken by another doomed detachment. In this way millions found their death, and present the world with a holocaust.

We have no record of what the victims may have said, but it is probable that the vast majority experienced here an event completely beyond their own understanding. They could not but manifest the tragic bewilderment which is expressed by the little girl who stood next to her mother, clutching a doll to the last. In the absence of recorded evidence we, the survivors, can only remotely enter into the experience of death at Auschwitz. We are in a position similar to that when we contemplate the death of Christ and countless martyrs. We observe first of all that this death cannot be equated with the common mortality of man. The knowledge that all men must die simply does not square with this death. The reason is not the physical phenomenon but the intention which causes death. Accordingly we rightly distinguish between death from natural and unnatural causes. The distinction does not arise so much from the fact that natural death is on the whole more civilized and probably less painful, but from the realization that the great issues of sin and guilt only arise in connection with murder. It is, therefore, of no help to cite those Biblical texts which speak of death itself as a haven and a source of relief, though we have no reason to doubt that once the bridge is crossed it is far better 'not to be'. Even at Auschwitz death must have been hailed as a relief by tens of thousands who could thus bid farewell to a wicked world of torment. But we cannot pounce upon this element of relief as a solution to our overpowering problem. In that respect Auschwitz bears some comparison with the cross of Christ, which no one hails as blessed because it freed Jesus from the world.

Similarly, Auschwitz extermination cannot be contained mentally by the very convictions about death which, as we have shown, were propagated and entertained by an important section of the victims. It is, for example, impossible to make out a case for the uniqueness of 'my death'. The whole method of extermination, the mechanism working on conveyor belt principles, rules out the majestic individuality of the personal death. It impresses upon all the old truth that in death we are all involved together. Here our flesh and breathing are the common denominator, and even our souls are right to the end thrown into the common pool, just as our corpses are burnt in the common incinerator. Death is not the great separator. I die with others, on my right and on my left. Nothing is left to chance, to private arrangements.

This way of death strips off the mask of the pretence of psychological explanations. It is not a world of dreams or an inward sickness. It is blunt enmity, in which the victors are those who are outside manipulating the machines. Their motivation is not 'psychological', but they are there for private advantage, an easy job. This realization rules out any mystification about this death. The intention is murderous, and there is no therapeutical explanation in terms of psychological analysis. Nothing can be made of this mass dying if man is the measure of all things, except the message of an anthropology of despair: the only thing that matters is to be outside, and not inside, the cage.

No doubt such despair prevailed among many. No doubt a burning hatred to the last remained the legacy of many.[1] Others knew, however inarticulately in the many languages assembled there, that they were witnesses to God, that they died for God, his law, the prophetic message, the wisdom from of old. They drowned their resentment in holding on to a transcendental cause. They could commit themselves to Truth with a 'It is finished' which espied the dawn, the beginning of a better age. The walk through gas and fire became in their intention the release not only from the body and its conditions, but from the murderous ruin. Even Auschwitz held and holds the secret of redemption. The final Credo bursts here all denominational ties and distortions. Man appears before God.

The vindication cannot take the usual forms. Like the victim of Golgotha these dead leave for the most part no children, no report, no property. Few of them leave even a name. Obscurity is the only memorial. Yet the transformation starts here also with the fulfilment of the Scriptures. In as much as they died innocently they became one with the suffering servant, the Israel of God. The Spirit seals their transitory lot with the stamp of eternal purpose.

Seen in this light Auschwitz becomes a spiritual challenge in which the visible phenomenon must be reinterpreted according to the great tradition of prophetic expectation and priestly ritual. Thus we escape from the purely tragic evaluation and negative despair. This holocaust is no less a sacrifice than that prefigured in the

[1] The evidence of Leo Baeck and others suggests, however, a notable absence of what we call hatred. On the other hand, Eugen Kogon, survivor of Buchenwald, states simply: 'The great majority of the men in the camps were filled with an unimaginable thirst for vengeance' (*The Theory and Practice of Hell*, p. 299).

Scriptures. Here again the circle closes, and the lives of the many are given for the sins of the world.

This acceptance of death as sacrifice was particularly experienced by those trained in the spiritual tradition of Judaism and Christianity. They never doubted the providential nature of their course. This heroic vision was brought to a fine point by a few martyrs who substituted themselves for others in going to death. In the terms of the Bible they regarded their lives as a ransom, their bodies as sin offerings, their death as redemptive.

By seeing their death within the cultic pattern they were transforming death itself. The mechanics of murder were turned into a Godward oblation. This spiritual achievement enabled them to 'die unto God', not as animals, caught up in the mechanics of slaughter, but with a freedom of self-giving. This power of transformation is itself a token of the divine Presence in death. The act of transformation shows the intimate connection between the work of the Spirit and the human will.

The basis of this transformation is God's love for man, given by the eternal promise in creation and redemption. It is not merely an ecstatic self-assertion of the higher self, or a feverish fantasy to meet a desperate situation, but the objectively grounded union with God which death cannot interrupt. It is not man at Auschwitz, but God who incorporates the terror into the pattern of meaningful sacrifice.

This meaning, however, is perceptible only to faith. It is grounded in the belief that God has himself entered human history in the sacrifice of Jesus. Thus the Church could interpret the death of Christ in terms of ancient ritual. Christ, the victim on the Cross, was seen as the high-priest from whom all sacrifice derives. Moreover, though killed once and for all, he was known to continue his priestly sacrifice eternally with God. Thus the tremendous themes of atonement were translated from temple ritual and annual observance to a celestial sanctuary where outside the limitations of man-made and temporal ceremonies he fulfils the whole cultic tradition. He who stood in need of no purification enters this sanctuary with his own blood to make restitution for the whole of mankind. The death of Jesus is therefore the very denial of an avoidable, though tragic, death, and his resurrection is more than the vindication of virtue. Rather the cosmic perfection depends upon his abiding work of sacrifice.

We can appropriate this pattern partly for the victims of Auschwitz, not in the sense that they are now gods or that their work aspired to perfection. No such claim can be made for any man, Christian, Jew, or devoutly virtuous members of other cults. The claim is that all these, at the point of life-giving, enter into the supreme sacrifice by way of a sharing analogy. As it was said that human rites before Christ prefigured his perfect consummation we now maintain that our holocausts are also deeply related thereto.

This argument may appear less difficult when we take the scapegoat motif from the day of atonement. The complicated ritual of Leviticus xvi summarizes not only Jewish but the whole human need to get rid of sin. Here survived an act by which the community solemnly and penitentially transferred its burden of guilt to the animal which was then taken to a cliff from which it was hurled to death, or to wander in the wilderness to take its load of sins to the home of the mystery of all evils, where it also died. Although not a few thinkers and pious leaders declared much of the institution of sacrifice to be of doubtful value, if not downright unnecessary and perverse, the core of the great need remained and demanded a sacrifice for sin.

The victims of the Nazi criminals were cast into this role of scapegoat. All the frustrations of the German people were seeking an outlet and found it in their own midst. The sins which were attributed to the Jews were precisely the sins which the nation knew itself to be guilty of. The Jews were accused of a shifty morality, of harbouring a corporate destructive intent, of a cowardly evasion of duty, of being aesthetically repellent. Looking now in cool detachment at the scene it is difficult to resist the generalizing judgment that these accusations were really self-accusations, now to be transferred to the victim. The passionate hatred, as has often been remarked, induced a strange identification between murderers and murdered, a blood tie, unconsciously sacrificial. To recall the scapegoat here is not a condonation of the venomous malice which enabled a whole people to offer another to die for its own sins. It is merely a citation of an important analogy which sets the incomprehensible within a framework which is psychologically not beyond our understanding to-day. But the psychological light is not redemptive, whereas the theological link may become so. It does not absolve the guilty of killing, but it accepts the place of the innocent in an act of universal identification. From the blood of Abel to the present day there runs a red thread of meaningful sacrifice through the history of men.

A further consequence of this identification focuses upon the resultant state of man. As St. Paul saw it, the removal of sin by God leads to a totally new evaluation of man. He is no longer the boastful fellow who requires self-justification and self-approval. Since death is seen in a new redemptive light of conquest it no longer proclaims defeat and shame. Now one of the worst consequences of a secular evaluation of Auschwitz has been, and still is, the apparent defeat of the innocent. There has been a feeling abroad that the shamefulness of their death is a stigma, not only to those who had a share in bringing it about, but also to the dead themselves. The sacrificial setting and our identification of the victims with Christ remove every stain of horror and obscure suspicions.

But these theological claims cannot get very far if they are mere fantasies spun by words. In this respect one must note not only the undoubtedly important psychological echo of our experience of the scapegoat, but also the experience of the Christian community. The death of Christ set forth as the perfect oblation was certainly not an esoteric absurdity but the heart of Christian existence from the start. It governed the Church's worship; although Eucharistic forms of worship varied from place to place they never failed to give the atoning death of Christ the central place in the liturgy. The living fellowship owed its all to him who after having been betrayed had taken bread and had anticipated his self-oblation by blessing, breaking, and sharing it. Similarly the cup of wine came to symbolize a share in his blood.

We do not know whether this meal was a Passover meal or not, but an intimate connection between the Lord's Supper and the Passover belongs to the earliest tradition. This adds a further insight into the meaning of Christ's death. If he dies in the manner of the Passover Lamb he sums up in his death the many traditions which the Passover retains to this day. Above all, it associates the death with liberation from Egyptian bondage, enabling every Israelite to say, as he must, 'I myself came out of Egypt'. The Passover background removes the barriers of space and time from Christ's death. With this background in mind the victim of Auschwitz may legitimately be set alongside the prototype of all suffering in the cause of righteousness. We may judge theologically that there is a great unity of suffering in the Sufferer who died for all men. The identification is irresistable.

Even more importantly, the Passover connection permits us to take the ancient strand of the sacred dance, the ecstasy of the night of the spring equinox, and the blood shed to ward off and placate the demonic, and weave it into our theme of redemptive suffering. Christ died to save mankind from its pagan madness. The victims of Auschwitz died because pagan madness wished to extirpate the light and to rule the world in dark, ecstatic nihilism. The cause of passing over from darkness into light is theirs, and they have consecrated it afresh in the modern struggle against the destroying forces and their dark works.

The ritual of the bitter herbs and sweet food accentuates the ambiguity of Passover. It is terrible and delightful, the Cross and Auschwitz reveal the depth of the darkness to be crossed, but the meal of the unleavened bread also brings out the deathlessness and joy of the communion of the Passover. It is not only a feast of remembrance, but also a firm resolution to have done

with darkness and despair. Though sacrificial, it is really
a feast, and the Christian is bidden to celebrate the feast
because 'Christ our Passover is sacrificed.' The casting
out of the leaven symbolizes the decisive ethical step not
to submit to natural fermentation and corruption. Thus
also the Cross and Auschwitz are not meant to hand on
to the future patterns of unending cruelty, but rather
the ending of the torment. Just because they have
endured to the end like sheep for the slaughter they plead
for the abolition of the malice and wickedness, the old
leaven of the old man.

Thus the Passover abolishes further killing and sets the
mind free from blood-lust and grim fantasies of horror.
Because the blood has been shed it cries out against the
reiteration of the same. The re-enactment of history in
the Passover does not inspire a philosophy of an eternal
return, as if the thing remembered must recur. On the
contrary it opens the vista to the future and leads the
people of God to press on to the end. The prophetic
apprehension of the Kingdom of God as the sole reality
of life lies at the farther end of the Passover sacrifice.
Thus even Auschwitz is set free from denoting only hell
on earth. It demands the end of the old, and the making
of the new, mankind.

We come to the dying Christ as we do to the dead of
Auschwitz with a restrained *De Profundis* in our hearts.
But we know we come to a place of transformation whose
heart is an altar with an atoning sacrifice. The priestly
understanding grows in its contemplation and adorns the
terrible gibbet, the camp, the gas chambers, the towers,
with praise and thanksgiving. The end must be the
beginning.

VIII

RESURRECTION

THE THEOLOGICAL DISCLOSURE endows Auschwitz with hope without denying the horror. It sets the whole reality of the camp within the total reality of creation and redemption and within the pattern of atonement. It can speak of glory where the shame cries out against mankind. It discerns a new type of corporate martyrdom, in which all sorts of individual destinies ended, where the whole vast complexity of the human condition was tried in an ordeal of transcendental dimensions.

None of the victims at Auschwitz wrought atonement. This was not the work assigned to them by God. Their purpose was to create new norms of martyrdom which fit into no known scheme of theology. Only a very few could bring personal perfection and readiness to their death. For them suffering was part of their life's work and they entered the atoning work of God by the imitation of the Servant, accepting the end with meek obedience and serenity. These are they who in robes of white innocence triumph and with unbroken fidelity enter life. If not in words they utter in deeds the timeless: *Ave Crux, Spes unica!* For them work and prayer blend in a disposition of love to the end. Like Bishop Ignatius of Antioch they greet the declining sun. They follow it with solemn joy in the wake of the eternal Light, the Christ, who was taken dead from the Cross and buried.

Not so the many, who in anxiety and deep sorrow leave this world, their minds in a disorder corresponding to the upheaval of the 'normal' scheme of things. They die to themselves in a way which no man can even enquire into. The dead at Auschwitz, however, died also for the sins of others, for in as much as they died there they took the place of all who could have died there, being morally culpable of the many causes which brought the horror into being. Their voices plead the cause of the unity of the whole human race. Not one life given there can cease to speak to the world as an accusation and as a warning. The dead of Auschwitz have risen from the dust. They proclaim not only their only ordeal and the wrong of the past. They address the present generation of scientists and moralists. They voice the challenge of sin and of righteousness, asking: 'Where are *you*? Who are *you*? Whither *your* way?' The legal files may close, but the moral quest grows in volume: '*Tua Res agitur!*', say the dead. 'Look to us, learn from us!'

The dead have risen up in the return of Israel from the diaspora. The creation of the State after heroic fighting would have been impossible but for the threat and the example of Auschwitz. This political achievement based upon military skill is the somewhat unsuspected consequence of the suffering of millions. It infuses a note of realism into the merely pious talk of resurrection. If it is resented by some as an unspiritual Zionism, a mere parody of the kingdom of God, let it be understood that Auschwitz no longer allows the division into practical and spiritual. Just as death was there designed in all its totality so now life must be viewed as one. But the rising from the ashes in the new Israel certainly confronts the

State and its secular society with a question mark. The new generation particularly must look to the quarry from which it was hewn, even if it does not like what it sees. The 'final solution' can never cease to remind Israel that its election as God's servant is no mean thing to be bartered away for advantages which accrue from being like the Gentiles. Israel, after Auschwitz, cannot discard the shadow of death. The *Churban* need not lie like a weight over the land, but as a constant reminder to Israel to be a light to the nations.

The dead have purified the air in which Israel lives, not only in the land, but in the whole world. No one who does not remember the ghettoes, the Christians' hatred for the Jews in central Europe, the suspicion, dislike, and contempt which surrounded the Jewish question even in countries not openly persecuting, can fully appreciate the new air of respect, and even liking, which the Gentiles and Negroes now feel for the Jews. It is as if the ice age had been succeeded by a new climate. Even if the non-Jews will not yet clutch the coat of a Jew to go with him to Jerusalem he will gladly receive him and start a dialogue with him, beneficial to both. The resolution of the Vatican Council on the Jews could never have been passed before Auschwitz—would that it had![1] The Lord's people are no longer accused of Deicide, a meaningless and yet nastily provocative

---

[1] Cf., for example, Appendix 3 to the new edition of the *Summa Theologica*, vol. 54, where St. Thomas is shown not to have been an Anti-Semite in his discussion of the causes of Christ's death. Pope John's 'I am Joseph, your brother' is contrasted with Hitler's hypocritical and unfounded appeal to Christian theology. See also the new wording of the Good Friday Liturgy in place of 'perfidious Jews' as formerly prayed.

charge. Jews and Christians form councils on which they
serve in a common cause. A great rapprochement has
taken place as a reply to the horrors of the past.

The corn of wheat which after so much torment fell
into the ground is thus bearing fruit which no one could
have predicted between 1942 and 1945.[1] How amazed
would be some of the dead if they saw that not only
Israel but Christianity also stands to benefit from the
burial! By ending the old hatred of the Jews and beginning to love the Jewishness of Christianity the Churches
may be said to enter upon a new epoch of their existence.
This is not the place to describe again the origin and
growth of Anti-Semitism in the Church. The scandal of
Judas-hating both led to Auschwitz and was redeemed
there. No Christian would now willingly wish to revive
the old embers of this hatred. Even in the backward
areas of Europe Christian belief can now be sustained
without the traditional scapegoat.

On the level of theological progress the Church cannot
but benefit from its recovery of dialogue with Israel.
Just because the Jews are no longer the scum fit for the
gas-ovens, bishops and rabbis can sit down together and
clarify important doctrinal differences. The Messiah's
status in Israel, the monotheistic tradition, and lesser
known aspects of Rabbinic Judaism, will throw a new
light upon Christian dogma. Difficulties in the texts of
the Old and the New Testament will be resolved more
easily by Hebraists of the Jewish faith. The ever-growing

[1] For example, in Germany alone, the work of the Ecumenical
Sisterhood of Mary at Darmstadt, led by M. Basilea Schlink, or the
Carmel of the Holy Blood on the site of the former concentration-
camp of Dachau.

intertestamental literature will elucidate the historical origins of Christianity with the help of Jewish scholarship.

The re-establishment of the dialogue will no longer be looked upon as the submission of one faith to the other. Nor will it be another instance of toleration and no more. The post-Auschwitz climate enables Christians to take seriously the Jewish position without for a moment belittling the claims of Christ and the Church. At the same time the extermination policy behind Auschwitz will never fail to remind Christians that the end of Judaism and the Jewish people must at length also involve the liquidation of Christianity and the Church. The organic unity and real diversity hold Judaism and Christianity in tension, but it is a wholesome, positive relationship, in theological thought as well as in practical existence.

The fruit-bearing of the corn of wheat does not stop in the religious sphere alone. The whole world is already coming under the influence of the resurrection from the torment. In the secular sphere on the stage, television, and in musical compositions a steady flow of creative works informs a new generation of these events. This is the modern equivalent of the tragedy which purges the heart with terror and pity. Pictures, too, both documentary and imaginary, confront the beholder, as did once the holy ikons and the stained glass windows, to solicit his sympathy in the cause of humanity. The intention behind this secular art is undoubtedly to re-enact the issue of Auschwitz as a warning, an example, and exhortation. There is, as it were, a Gospel of Auschwitz to be proclaimed to every generation. But the arts do not preach it openly, since this is not their business. It is enough to engage the spectator's feelings so that he can identify himself with the cause of innocent suffering and humiliation. The living, thus touched, enter into a legacy bought with blood.

This legacy, resurrected from the ashes, is a humanitarian Credo. It assents to the belief that human life is sacred and that no racial, credal, or social differences may be permitted to cause discord among men. It furthermore disowns the indifference towards political institutions and economic realities which provides fuel for the fires of a new Auschwitz. Hence it is a legacy of cool and deliberate responsibility. This humanitarian attitude does not despise an intelligent assessment of real problems. Auschwitz is no excuse to fight again old battles in order to avoid new ones. The population explosion, taken in conjunction with nuclear weapons, obviously exceeds in its problematic structure even the apparently insoluble issues of the first half of the twentieth century. The legacy of Auschwitz does not pretend that it can offer a solution here, but it can and must shout from the tops of mud-huts or sky-scrapers that men are brothers. The final solution of inhuman murder is no solution but suicide of all.

But the message from Auschwitz has a right to warn that these new problems are not rendered harmless by fine words. The hypocrisy of lip-service, as expressed in clichés, must yield to a less superficial treatment. The slogan of brotherhood is no less suspect when it appears in its humanitarian, rather than its theological or moral, guise. If the principles of humanism and of theological ethics are nowadays seen to be closer to each other, the resurrection from the *Churban* challenges both in the terms of Ezekiel, chapter xxxvii: 'Can these bones live?' In contemporary language: 'How can you give teeth to pious phrases?' The quest raises again the matter which generations before Auschwitz chose to ignore with such dire consequences, namely, by whose authority and with what power can anyone maintain that might is not stronger than right? Thus the agreed syllabus of right action looks again to the transcendental issue. The dust of Auschwitz posits the Law, not without the Lawgiver, the prophetic ideal, not without the authority of the Spirit, the Wisdom, not without the Word which is Reason. Just because these ideals existed before Auschwitz and foundered so tragically, the present necessity dare not go around the hard core and ignore the source of the authority which alone makes these ideals viable.

It seems to me at this point that the resurrection of the seed buried at Auschwitz lacks in power. Without a doubt the *Churban* pleads the helplessness of man as against the evil intent of the robot clad in black. Even if we choose not to accept the notion that a demonic power exists in the world, and resent the notion that the killing power of some decades ago is bracing itself for a renewed onslaught of total destruction, it is difficult to see how the mechanical engine can be stopped from falling into, what we are pleased to call, the wrong hands. The legacy of Auschwitz is a constant warning against relativity and tolerant judgments in matters of human conduct. It asserts the unpopular division into right and wrong, sheep and goats, actions to be approved and to be condemned. The ethics of the commandments, for all their brevity, establish a norm from which not only principles, but also authority and power, are derived.

The legacy of this resurrection is a return to the Lord of Law and Order.

This Law is not to be decried as 'cold legalism', but to be recognized as the universal, binding, and dynamic force which is greater than human society. Its authority is not at an end when men violate it. The ancient instinct to preserve order and to keep chaos at bay is, after Auschwitz, made into a conscious responsibility. It is the scientific equivalent to the mystical apprehension that this order was created as the outpouring of the divine creativity. The earth is the microcosm which reflects the pattern of the macrocosm, and this correspondence gives the law an authenticity which transcends human opinion and expediency. Thus the sacredness of life, the duty to parents, the inviolability of monogamous marriage, the significance of property, can now be evaluated as necessary to the maintenance of human dignity. But this dignity is itself right and proper because it is authorized by the divine order. With this link broken, not only in theology but also in practical matters, all restraints will go and despite lip-service to peace and humanity, another and worse Auschwitz will come. Without the sovereignty of God the natural law ultimately fails to prevail, and man stripped of duty and privileges appears again naked, ready for the conveyor belt leading to destruction.

The aftermath of Auschwitz cannot tolerate an easy truce, plastered over with ideals without authority. The universal pattern of order requires, however, not only the signatures of the millions, but also its constant prophetic interpretation. Laws without the ecstatic element fail. Amos, Hosea, Isaiah, Micah, and Jeremiah inspired 'here and now' decisions, rebukes, teachings, in a tone so elevated that it bestowed authority. The universal Word has been thus transmitted, gathering up into itself the historical experiences of many ages and races. Auschwitz lends it a renewed solemnity. The residue of the dust gives to the last a new impetus. Righteousness becomes a force greater than forensic justice. The ecstatic acclamation of the 'torrents' of eternal and creative right directs men to goodness and stirs them into enthusiasm. 'Seeking good and resisting evil' is lifted from a somewhat priggish background or pecksniffian censoriousness. It means personal decision.

The resurrection from Auschwitz unites our private decisions with the public sector. The 'I' and the 'We' are distinct and yet inseparable. Thus the prophetic ideal, without which this world must perish, becomes meaningless as a statement in abstract terms. Perfectionism, as the ideals before Auschwitz have shown, is its own undoing if no one can come anywhere near fulfilling it. As the mechanization of culture and society proceeds an even greater emphasis must be given to personal responsibility in the corporate life.

The post-Auschwitzian decision is, therefore, not unlike that of the early Christian Church. It faces tremendous odds which make victory unlikely. Yet it boldly faces the Goliath machine of the state with the unarmed confidence of young David. In order to sustain this struggle it relies upon discipline, a training in battle. Pre-Auschwitz suffered not from an insufficiency of ideals, but from a pathetic absence of ascetic. The idealists had not sat down to calculate the cost, nor the means of implementing grandiose plans. After Auschwitz we know that enthusiasm is not enough. The ecstatic element left to itself may become positively evil or just a nuisance. The prophetic tradition transforms the religious temperament into a reliable force only if body and mind are 'kept under'. Whereas much modern theology seems to despise the ancient ways of prayer the dust from Auschwitz elevates mortifications, and all ways of concentration, absorption, and contemplation, to the highest level. The unrelenting pressure of the picture of the SS before us still compels serious training in physical and spiritual resistance. It completely excludes a cheap way of salvation, without effort and constant preparation. Thus even the military vocabulary, which used to speak in terms of the helmet of salvation and the breastplate of righteousness and the sword of the spirit, still avails in this age of guns, bombs, and missiles. The armament is not in slogans, such as 'moral rearmament', but in the practice of the highest form of the unitive way, the God-in-us realization in this present world.

Without this personal response the Resurrection must remain sterile and the dust will settle without hope. This hope, as almost all would agree, centres in the valid re-establishment of love as the direct antithesis to the hell from which we are to rise. The nucleus of this love was never extinguished by physical death or torment. Being the cause of the creation and its sustaining power and the destiny of the universe, Love confronts the generations after Auschwitz as the transcendent, miraculous, indispensable Unknown. Never before has God as Love been felt more keenly necessary and yet inaccessible as in the computer-governed process of living. Auschwitz appears as the huge perversion of the human race because of the triumph of hatred. The absence of all grace and mercy is the great confirmation that life without grace and mercy is impossible for the human kind. But Auschwitz issues also the warning that the divine gift is as precious as in the past and not part of the mechanism of existence. It is, given the circumstances, easier to hurl babies into an oven than to look after them by hiding them and feeding them. The sharing of food, the caring for the sick, the identification with the other man, demands a firm stance in the divine covenant where grace is received for grace to be given.   *

The resurrection from Auschwitz is, therefore, still more a demand than a given fact. The test of its reality is, as after the resurrection of Christ, the love of the brethren as shown by the deep interchange of mercy. Earthly acts of mercy, as Auschwitz has shown, are mirrors of eternal Grace. They demand not only the training in continual awareness but a restraint of self. Just as Hosea connected merciless promiscuity with adultery and 'not knowing God', and proceeded to practise mercy by reflecting the divine faithfulness, in order to 'redeem' his wife, so the 'good man' at Auschwitz, and the risen man after Auschwitz, curbs the blind desires of self-gratification in favour of the flow of that Grace which stands beyond duty and custom. The experience of the twentieth century agrees, therefore, with the New Testament tradition that Grace and Love, as savoured in mercy, are not optional extras, which the rich can, for example, pass on to the less fortunate, but the *sine qua non* of human existence. The tradition of Grace and free will attains to its full stature in a world where the machines will run on and on, burning, gassing, maiming, or even just entertaining. Only the will which reflects divine mercy can master this appalling power.

Resurrection from Auschwitz can never mean abolition of suffering. Rather it integrates suffering as the touchstone of true experience. Our sensitivity to pain, which induces us to take avoiding action wherever possible to physical and mental suffering, registers a whole scale of degrees of suffering. But this apparently endless and ever-growing total of suffering is to be freed from its meaningless, and therefore horrible, ache.

Christian theology is, sometimes rightly, suspected of circumventing the tragic nucleus too soon and too easily. It may reach out to the Resurrection too superficially, as if to leave behind the cross and the smoke from the chimneys. Its instinct is in line with all human feeling for comedy. Thus Jaspers, for example, refuses to find the true tragic reality in a religion which appeals to a 'Risen One'. At Athens greatness of character was set forth in terms of catastrophe. The spectators were not purged by Resurrection but by accepting the terrible with resignation.

Auschwitz compels us to incorporate the tragic reality in the redemptive process. Resurrection is not the easy way out, but the validation of the tragic itself. This paradox is not new to a religion which portrays the Risen One with wounds in hands and feet and side. Resurrection does not obliterate the marks of tragedy but translates them from the level of passing incident to that of eternal worth. Auschwitz is overcome not by tragic resignation but by victory over impersonal and meaningless torment in personal love.

This climax of Resurrection stands beyond tragedy, but since it demands the transcendence of self-interest it involves suffering. Self-transcendence, as Tillich affirms, cannot but be 'tragic'.[1] Yet the terror and the pity of the tragic are now set within the divine creation and redemption. Auschwitz loses its isolation because God has raised Christ from the dead.

The deliverance from Auschwitz, which we would celebrate as Resurrection, is not a return to private suffering or private enjoyment, nor the sanction for private security. We do not return to our base to gain an unassailable plot in the present world. Resurrection is a celebration of new things and an anticipation of new life. This corporate event touches the whole stream of human aspirations. It is the spiritual proclamation of anti-Auschwitz, made and heeded by the enemies of the old order of destruction.

The tragic content of our age converges upon the Other. The 'dead God' of the century whom the people worship has been exposed. The 'living God' rises among the dead as the Lord of glory and mercy. The Resurrection from Auschwitz brings union with his eternal being not only in the direct experience of the Other but also in the conscious and abiding participation in his objective Being.

The adoration of God is the ground and goal of this resurrection. It provides the objective, cultic, and personal reality in and outside the camp of death. There remains a Sabbath for the people of Auschwitz, whose sufferings are now within the pattern of creation and redemption. Our memorial sets forth the life and death

[1] *Systematic Theology*, vol. 3, pp. 98–100.

of a people in common with the great liturgy of him who Is, because he died and rose again from the dead. Thus the congregation are freed from only sorrowing in remembrance but creatively sanctify the future by the Spirit. The deliverance from Auschwitz is not resurrection without liturgical expression. The triumphant Gloria sets it within the framework of mankind's longing for salvation and the divine Amen.

IX

ASCENSION AND REGENERATION

WE HAVE so far defied the opposition of dialectical materialism and of dubious theology. We have taken the radical despair of an extreme human situation in history and endeavoured to interpret it in the light of the suffering Christ. We have also looked at the aftermath of the holocaust as reflected in the triumph of the Crucified One. We have mingled our catastrophe with his way and work, sometimes beginning with what is recorded of him, sometimes with the facts of the near-contemporary scene. We gained the advantage of eliminating the gulf of time. By holding up the mirror of Auschwitz before Golgotha we removed the veil of unreality from the latter; by contrasting Golgotha with Auschwitz we brought the latter into a wider reality and gave spiritual meaning to the meaningless. By this interplay of tragic destiny and historical realities we endeavoured to knit our existence to both, not in order to establish a morbid fondness for death but in order to recall ourselves to moral duties and spiritual glories.

We believe, therefore, to have shown that Christian tradition and present experience fertilize one another and that neither of them can be segregated unless cynical despair is to overtake us all. The secular account of secular events is no account at all. Auschwitz demonstrates that neither economic nor political factors make up a full explanation of the event. The evil is multi-dimensional, ranging from impersonal mechanical techniques to personal will-power directing human organizations. An objective analysis of Auschwitz will never lose out of sight these 'secular facts', but it will also insist that the quality of the phenomenon demands a more-than-secular understanding.

The shortcomings of a purely secular account are not academic. It twists and distorts the record for new purposes of propaganda, and in this re-writing of history the sufferings of the past suffer anew from lies. Thus Communist accounts blot out, for example, the Jewishness of the martyrdom in order to buttress the thesis of the class-war, insinuating even that all Capitalist powers were equally to blame.[1] But even in the absence of deliberate bias the secular account fails because it cannot rescue the event from oblivion. As the generation of survivors dies the blanket of forgetfulness is spread over this and many other issues. Indifference has the last word.

By turning an episode in history into a unique, one might say, sacred cause, we take a step of great trans formation. We claim that God reigns throughout the catastrophe and dismiss the pessimistic view, expressed by Emerson, that 'things are in the saddle and ride mankind.' We venture to attribute the glory of the ascended Christ to the gassed millions. We deny that the dead are dead still. We oppose the cynical thesis that all things remain as they have always been and that it is best

---

[1] Cf., for example, Peter Weiss, *Revisiting Auschwitz*, and discussion of his work and views in *Encounter* 1965. Soviet anti-Jewishness persistently distorts the past.

to be a guard rather than a prisoner, to eat well rather than to starve in the godless circus.

The task before us is to release the evidence of transcendent reality. It has been met in the past and at present in great art. The poet can take the dead by the hand, as it were, and lead them to Elysian fields and feed them on ambrosia and nectar. He can invoke the glory of the departed who come out of tribulation in white robes. His words transform the meanness of death into the joy of ever-lasting life. 'Blessed are the dead', in all its forms of true feeling, is the theme of inspiration which dwells on the deathless state.

Nor is this reality of the Ascension confined to words. The music of the spheres of immortal life is already part of our experience. Freedom and joy light up like sparks of God's presence the dark paths as the strings, woodwinds, trumpets and percussion intone the triumph over death. How infinitely small appear our torments as the eternal harmony resolves them in heaven!

Even visual imagery and sculpture help us to acclaim the new life. Death is portrayed, not as the end, but as the gateway to endless life in circles of ascending light. Even the spring sunshine and the cornfields before the harvest adumbrate only the lowest rung on the ladder of ascent. All life is seen to return to the fount and origin, without weight or hindrance.

Thus art accomplishes our release from the grip of death through the power of the Ascension.[1] But where is the theological liberation flowing from the same source?

Auschwitz is, therefore, a challenge to modern theology and to the confession that 'to fail here is to fail

[1] For a detailed treatment see my *The Ascent to Heaven*, 1961.

everywhere'.[1] Unless God can be seen to bring reconciliation to the irreconcilable, to make man's lost cause
and ruin his own and gain, the here and now casts its
spell over the future as well as over the past. Without
the great transcendental 'Nevertheless' non-existence
overtakes being. Theology, so long a prisoner to history
and earthly evidence, must step out of its secular walls.
The Science of the Cross is also the Science of the
Resurrection whose central Nevertheless 'Now is Christ
risen from the dead' judges our non-existence and transforms the human condition of death into eternal life. It
counters Auschwitz with the miraculous, the discon-
tinuous, the There and Then which is known by the
Spirit. Auschwitz discounts the theology of earthly
evidence and demands the disclosure given from above.

This demand stresses the subtle relationship between
the believer and his faith. We are critically aware of the
dangers of make-belief. A projection of our hopes is not
rooted in fact. Hence we repudiate the kind of faith
which provides a leap into faith, a mystical cutting of
the knot of all our problems. An existentialist decision
raises no one from the dead. Only He Who Is, God,
creates and sustains such an order of things as fulfils the
aspirations of the believer's hopes. The God of Auschwitz
is not made in the image of our despair, but rather meets
our despair by his total Otherness and Reality. He is not
the ground of our rotten and rotting being, but the
Ground of what we are not and must yet become.

The transcendental 'Nevertheless' is, therefore, always

---

[1] Karl Barth, *Church Dogmatics*, IV/1, p. ix on the Atonement.
He also states the obverse: 'To be on the right track here makes it
impossible to be completely mistaken in the whole.'

known in our repudiation of sin and unreality, which is
the first step in faith. To say 'No' to Auschwitz is already
to say 'Yes' to our ascent in faith, hope, and love. With
Luther we may state the common experience that unless
we had perished we should not have believed. Thus the
work of the divine Grace arises within the camp's walls.
There we realize not only what we are, but also what we
may become because God is and acts.

The extreme situation of mankind, hanging over the
precipice, is not helped by an attenuated Christianity in
which Christ figures only as the man par excellence. The
dying body, the buried corpse, the disciples' memory,
and all the other stages of his earthly life, only enhance
the ambiguity of our existence. His humility might have
been lack of courage; his obedience the result of an inner
helplessness. The man Jesus, enclosed in time and space,
is one of millions of sufferers who did not solve the in-
superable task of blending an ideal with success in this
life. His teaching oscillates between an unworkable
perfectionism and a passive resignation. His death is tied
up with the administrative convenience of the age and
does not defeat it. Our interpretation of it, whether in
legal, financial, military, or cultic terms, remains still
earth-bound, as we have seen. As long as he stands in
our place only because he really belongs to us as one of
us, in Jewish flesh, under Pontius Pilate, he cannot
escape from the 'was-ness' of his place.

It is, therefore, not surprising that even now we are
without atonement for, and victory over, Auschwitz.
Only from the standpoint of eternity can the temporal
impasse be surmounted. Jesus the pre-existent Word and
the ascended Lord gives validity to the redemption of

the irredeemable. Christ is neither one of the Titans who defies God with the resolution of Prometheus, nor one of us who leads the way out of suffering. He is the Son of God who transmuted the Cross not only by what he did and suffered but also because he was what he is: God. Similarly he did not rise from the dead to leave an enigmatic empty tomb and to create a myth of resurrection, but he ascended to be with God as the eternal mediator. He neither was nor is partner of the human condition only, but rather he has taken and takes the human condition into his divinity.

Our humanity depends on the divinity of the incarnate Lord as the assurance of the meaningfulness of the meaningless. Without the God-Man Auschwitz would stand as a nightmare, the culmination of unreason and malice. Owing to his divine status alone there is no suffering which remains outside the orbit of meaning mediated by him: 'In order to atone for the sins of all men Christ suffered the most profound sadness, but not so great that it exceeded the rule of reason' (St. Thomas Aquinas, S.T.Q. 46).

The transformation of suffering by Christ even admits joy to the pain. There is a spiritual fruition in the passion which qualifies his suffering. It occurs in the right place, at the right time, for the right cause, because he is Lord. His death transforms death itself because he dies uniquely, retaining his identity at every stage. He who was conceived of the Virgin Mary is still the same who sees no corruption in the tomb and whose manhood is eternally presented in his ascended state.

Now this absence of corruption and the conquest of death by the One who acts for the many, so that they may share the Glory which he enjoyed from before the beginning, enables us at last to say that the dead are not dead because they have been gassed and their bodies burnt in crematoria. Here the miracle of the Crucified extends beyond compassion and tentative identification: the ascended state is the guarantee also of a blessed future beyond the total perversion and nothingness. Our existence over the precipice discovers the 'other possibility', the transcendental 'and yet', the interchange that God became man so that man may become united to God.

But this timeless, universal, and cosmic conception of Christ's work spells out not only the possibility of life but also discloses the totality of human guilt. The human disorder is what it is because it deludes itself with its own self-governing autonomy. Christ, having given himself to the depth of the most utter helplessness, proclaims in his exalted state the unlimited shame of the human condition and its total regeneration by Grace. Man's wrong and man's pardon no longer lie on the periphery of some special concern, such as religion provides, but at the heart of all earthly existence. The redemptive act by the Holy Spirit begins with God's self-attestation in Christ and takes effect in our naked trust that what he has done is available to us. The threat of Auschwitz is met not by the great deterrent, nor made good by vindictive measures and retribution; rather it is overcome by rising with the Risen, ascending to the Ascended.

The Ascended Christ authorizes the transformation of all things human, whether they be institutions, memories, or fears. His Alpha of pre-cosmic unity with God and his Omega of lifting humanity to God harness the Cross to the eternal pattern of reality. From this there flows the assurance of forgiveness. Auschwitz need not be forgotten—indeed, how could it be?—but can now be forgiven, because the torment has not only ceased but is established in the divine life itself. We have now the answer to Ivan Karamazov's apparently impregnable position of despair, for revenge and resentment are taken out of our hands. In as much as we ourselves seek forgiveness with the tormented, and thus enter into the life-cycle of guilt and atonement, we become the recipients of the God-for-Us mercy. In our response to it we remember the whole past through the light of forgiveness.

Modern theology rightly stresses the experience of forgiveness, though it errs when it attempts to isolate the experience from him who grants and authorizes it in his state of ascended glory. The forgiveness is the work of the Holy Spirit in us, imparted by God through Christ ascended and interceding on our behalf. It is not a psychological resolution on our part to pardon ourselves and others. Its supernatural and miraculous quality is vouchsafed by all the natural reasons which speak against an amnesty. The transforming power of forgiveness also derives entirely from its divine origin. It does not yield the peace and temporary consolation which false appeasement and mental therapy so often provide. Rather it evokes a transcendental peace which, as Jesus insisted, is 'not of this world'. It is known analogously by healing in sickness, fresh showers after a long drought, children after a period of barrenness. But the analogy emphasizes in the 'how-much-more' of the act of Grace the unique regenerative power of forgiveness in the soul.

This act of forgiveness acts upon us in our earthly

situation. It undoes the past and its terrors. It opens up channels of reconciliation, turning foe and fiend into friend and ally. Yet of the supernatural quality nothing is sacrificed, since without Grace forgiveness is impossible. It rests upon the union of the faithful with God and his act of forgiveness. When Edith Stein is known after her martyrdom to intercede lovingly for ex-SS men and their families we recognize that forgiveness not only by miraculous events on earth but by its celestial quality.[1]

Transformation by forgiveness is not a mythical ideal, if the challenge of the slave-state and its outrages is met by God. The complete abolition of Grace in the godless organization is then confronted by the freedom of men under Grace. The transformation of Auschwitz is the modern symbol of this transcendent hope. It is already achieved in the accomplished atonement, but it is yet to be consummated on earth.

This problem of transformation was in the past solved by the attempt to rule the world. Even in Israel the transcendent hope was vested in the lawful institution. A good king among a dedicated people stood for the Messianic ideal. Yet the history of Israel refuted the practicability of the ideal. After the exile it was restated in more cautious terms: the secular and the religious power were to transform the general misery by sharing authority. Similarly the Church tried to mediate the reign of the Ascended Christ in the pagan world, by assuming the control of the state in the first place, and accepted the donation of Constantine. Later Church

[1] Cf. *Edith Stein, Eine Heilige?*—testimonies written in connection with the hope that she will be canonized.

and State agreed to wield the two swords of spiritual and secular authority. After Auschwitz all such endeavours to consummate the power of Christ by ruling over Anti-Christ have ceased to operate, except in a few isolated pockets of Church dominion. Indeed the churches themselves no longer express a belief in a secular dominion to transform the world.

A withdrawal from direct power may release spiritual reserves as in the past. Traditional other-worldliness has achieved a great deal in the world. Churches, schools, colleges, hospitals, colonized swamps and cleared jungles, bear witness to the efficacy of the other-worldly, self-effacing, Christ-work. In this tradition the transformation of the world is achieved indirectly and often unwittingly. Yet these works of piety often succumb to the power of the slave-state which either takes over the institution and property by force or changes its character by infiltration. Thus the secular arm grows stronger and longer in its hold on freedom-asserting institutions. At its worst, we watch the process of transformation in reverse, i.e., the subjugation of the spirit by administrative rule.

In the post-Auschwitz world the freedom of the spirit is more easily preserved by the incognito permeation of the secular world. Even in the early part of the twentieth century Christians felt a vocation to work out the transcendent Grace in the given fields of education, social services, industry, and politics. In the English-speaking world at least this penetration of the hard world of secular institutions by the so-called social Gospel has been amazingly successful, but even at its most startling the process of transformation always loses something of the specifically transcendent reflection of God. The problem of the transformation of public life, or the anonymous IT, by the involvement of responsible persons in this life, nevertheless pinpoints the enormous possibilities of personalizing the IT in living I-Thou relationships.

Two criticisms against this involvement deserve to be noted. One comes from the side of spiritual integrity. Thus the worker-priests in France were, perhaps unjustly, condemned for their trend towards a secularization in which once again the transcendent suffered irremediable loss. The second comes from the secularists who suspect an ulterior motive in religious infiltration. Even when genuine and not out for 'results' the social Gospel seems to the sociologist naive if it deems itself capable of substituting good will for hard work in day-to-day legislation. The spiritual attitude is accused of evading the hard core of real conflicts, whether in the field of wage negotiations or racial violence. Wars, concentration-camps and the like, steam-roller this kind of private enterprise into the mud.

This two-edged criticism proves that transformation requires more than good-will and liberal abundance. We have to accept the fact that there are no reserves. The problem of transformation is not solved by a *de haut en bas* attitude. The needed miracle is, after all, not a gesture of wealthy moralists who can afford to 'give a helping hand'. The freedom of God is to flow among men yet to be made free.

No wonder that the modern prisoner recoils from all institutional commitments and being driven to the opposite extreme looks for the ascent to heaven in his private world and nowhere else. All social links bring their restrictions. Meetings are fortuitous and passing. Even if they are not offensive other people are in the first place our enemies. This existentialist thesis moves from the pure economic feeding-trough experience to the disillusionment caused by love. The transformation which we suffer through other people is never divinely transcending, except in the rare moments of ecstatic identification. But even then we transcend ourselves only in order to find a mirror of ourselves, or a target for our needs.

The logic of existentialism is irrefutable. It locates the freedom for transformation in the individual. Like Kafka's K. the existentialist proceeds into the castle of his own consciousness. There he can ignore the world. He can remain free even at Auschwitz by erecting a fence around himself to fence in his freedom in slavery. Outside Auschwitz the Organization Man cannot touch him. He touches life at the point where he contracts out of life.

The modern hermit, like his traditional forbear, adjusts himself to conditions, but does not transform them. As he stands on his own pillar he makes a bid for his own transformation. His endeavour is as heroic as the social ways of perfection. His freedom is not sapped by secularization and institutionalization, but it is not the freedom gained by the Cross of 'other people' which comes to fruition here. It is a transcendent answer to Auschwitz, but it is not the freedom of the ascension.

Yet the failure of the ways of self-transcendence by the sword, by the build-up of institutions, by the permeation of the secular world, and by retrenchment for personal

decision, only indicates the magnitude of the task of
transformation. All these ways are valid, but none
achieve their end, for the vocation of man transcends
world and self. 'The Word of the living Jesus Christ is
the creative call by which he awakens man to an active
knowledge of the truth and thus receives him into the
new standing of the Christian, namely, into a particular
fellowship with Himself, thrusting him as his afflicted but
well-equipped witness into the service of His prophetic
work.'[1]

Transformation, then, is the work of God among men
called 'before the foundation of the world', inseparable
from community in history, from relationships with all
their contradictions. It is quantitatively immeasurable
and it is qualitatively unique. God himself transforms
the world through his Spirit and the prophet stands in
the world as the living sign of this creative and redemptive work. In his call and obedience in freedom he
receives the transforming power.

This conception of ascent is both sudden and gradual.
The call through illumination converts the will and
coincides with the rebirth as in a flash; the renewal and
preservation of man, however, occur in several stages
of pilgrimage. The experience of the prisoner in the face
of death and liberation confirms the dramatic and also
the timeless nature of transformation. The tangible signs
of the ascent, in speech, deed, ecstasy, and suffering,
occur as events in time, but they are what they are only
in manifesting God's eternal purpose. Hence the service
to the world and the existentialist decision are taken up
beyond time and space, for in the Auschwitz situation

[1] Karl Barth, *Church Dogmatics*, Summary of Par. 71.

the epiphany of God takes precedence over what we do and decide to be.

By putting epiphany before action we are, however, exposing ourselves to a renewed onslaught of selfish quietism. Are we perhaps overcoming the challenge of history once again by evading our responsible part? Are we content to keep our visions and virtues to ourselves? Are we in danger of underestimating the intrinsic worth of achievement in history? The man after Auschwitz cannot quote too often from 'Measure for Measure':

> Heaven does with us as we with torches do,
> Not light them for themselves. For if our virtues
> Did not go forth of us, 'twere all alike
> As if we had them not.

The 'one glass of water' symbolizes for us a good intention, a good work achieved, an epiphany in darkness, a community of mercy in the merciless unfolding of historical power. Clearly, then, it is a theological duty to uphold 'good works', not only because they derive from faith, but for their intrinsic worth, great or small. Otherwise it is difficult to see why the work of Christ, the works of the Christians, beginning with the Acts of the Apostles, should not be consigned to the same realm of oblivion where history is overcome by total silence, the great unconscious. These vast forces are potentially always ready to swallow up or freeze the evidence of human endeavour and divine creativity among men, and it is only through the disclosure of the eternal in time that the great transformation can rise above the dust of entropy which envelops all.

Our theological conclusion, therefore, must be against all the deceits of progress, the lures of a social Gospel, the worship of culture, and the evasion of quietism. The regeneration through the ascended Christ spills over into these external and inward spheres of the complex human situation, without ever terminating the process of transformation; but the Kingdom of God can never 'be' on earth. The expectation provides the dialectic between eternity and history, but it does not lessen the reality of both. Rather, the tension makes such demands as can only be met by human decisions which go beyond their immediate terms of reference. Tillich is right when he discerns in the ultimate concern the authority for temporal decisions with eternal significance. Only thus actions qualify for the 'history of salvation'.

We therefore conclude, in the light of Auschwitz and the Biblical tradition, that all attempts to sever faith from works, to the detriment of either, show a complete disregard for the divine revelation and for human experience. Their unity, in fact, constitutes the truth. At Auschwitz every attempt at order and humanity is a signal of the faith which is being crushed. After Auschwitz, every endeavour for freedom, taken at the level of hard work and responsible decision, still points to the divine will. Similarly, every frustration suffered, every defeat incurred in this endeavour, takes us back to the Cross which inspires the action.

But the clue to this unity must be found neither in abstractions, such as faith and works, but rather in concrete and personal witness. 'The Christian who is called by God in Jesus Christ through the Holy Spirit, exists in an apparently endless multiplicity of different forms

in his specific freedom, orientation, and determination.'[1]
Because of this endless multiplicity Barth rightly insists
that we must locate the concrete controlling principle
behind this witness. All answers which make the witness
relative to human needs, and, even worse, depend upon
human possibilities, drag the role of the witness into a
morass of short-lived and ultimately meaningless actions.
Even the distinction between worldliness and other-
worldliness cannot suffice, as if only the other-worldly
were proper witness. Even a so-called Christian ethos
falls short of the issue. The true answer lies with the
witness himself: who having died to sin has risen to
righteousness like his Master, and who therefore is in the
world like Christ.

Now the interpretation of this life in Christ cannot be
reduced to a common denominator, such as the enjoyment of the blessings of Christ, or the proclamation of his
Gospel, or the following in his footsteps, although these
and many other definitions will at the right time be
right. But the role of the witness is always controlled by
his concrete task: a pure and genuine task laid upon the
witness.[2] God makes him his witness in action and in
inaction, unknown to the world, hidden often to himself.

Regeneration, then, is not obtained cheaply, as, for
example, by publicity. All theological schools agree with
the Bonhoeffer dictum that Cheap Grace is the counter-
feit of discipleship. The witness cannot even opt out of a
history which he detests. To denounce Babylon, or
Auschwitz, is a matter of taste, words, or moral conviction; but to stand against it, and for God through

[1] K. Barth, C.D., IV/3, p. 554.
[2] ibid., esp. p. 575.

God, is the test of the genuine vocation. Man's regeneration is inseparable from his obedience to the divine commission. One might say, God signs him because he responds to be God's sign in the world. What Barth calls 'the fellowship of action' determines the prophetic witness. It is 'the strange work' which Isaiah ascribed to God and carried out himself. With the greatest theological caution one may therefore speak of co-operation with God by the fellow-workers.

At this stage the theologian is apt to insert a thousand qualifications by which he hedges around Christian witness—and perhaps kills it. Nevertheless, it must be stressed that this conception of prophetic work differs in all essentials from 'good work'. It is not the upshot of spare moral capacity or psychological need. Again the mirror of Auschwitz helps to show the radical difference between 'spare capacity' and obedience. But when this difference is acknowledged it may then be asserted without too much timidity that this prophetic witness is not a clerical, ecclesiastical, denominational or any other preserve and its sphere is not restricted by religious bounds. If 'religionless Christianity' and 'secular Christianity' are not used as an excuse to evade this razor's edge of vocation at its most traditional, even these labels may help to disclose the majesty of Grace and the infinite scope for mercy set forth personally in an impersonal and merciless world.

The Christian then stands in the world, for the world, and against the world. Tradition and experience show us that no one fares alike in this way of witness. Only one common denominator is alike to all: they die and they live, they show forth the death and the resurrection of

Christ. In this respect, however, the human inclination is an uncertain guide. The normal preference for, what may roughly be called, prosperity or success stands over against the abnormal longing for martyrdom, in the technical sense. The generosity of the young Christian— young not only in age, but in zeal—cannot conceive of Christian service apart from loss and self-sacrifice. But this prophetic extremism is not generally nourished by the institutional life of the Church, which reckons in terms of growth and advance. Thus a conservative, and even preservative, weight more than out-balances the individual readiness 'to die for Christ', if only by making the reasonable plea that 'to live for Christ' is more demanding in the long run. Thus the argument easily short-circuits and leads to sterile controversies between enthusiasts and anti-enthusiasts. In practice we are left with phrases such as 'soldiers of Christ' who never come off the drawing-board. Indeed, the singing of 'Fight the good fight' may easily hide the truly militant ingredient of witness. Auschwitz, at any rate, shows how hopelessly Christendom can go astray in its muddle over vested institutional rights and personal heroism. The Church as a community did not fight the good fight, but left the witness to the few. Similarly to this day the big machine is concerned with its own survival and administration, while the witness is left to individual, and even eccentric, efforts. But the true tradition of witness must transcend human inclination and political expediency.

The good confession of Christ, then, is found neither in a retreat from a clash with the world, nor in an imprudent and fanatical self-sacrifice to the world. Edith Stein at Auschwitz perpetuates the true Christian-

Jewish position better than any verbal definition. Her removal from Cologne to Echt in Holland on December 31st, 1938, stands for the extreme care taken in not jeopardizing a life for nought. Her readiness to go to Switzerland, if possible, re-enacts the prayer—and hoped-for reality—of 'let this cup pass from me!' Her arrest and journey to Auschwitz at length seals the 'Thy will be done!'

The true witness has no desire to provoke this 'baptism of blood'; history has shown, in rather an absurd way, how self-imposed martyrdom discredits the claims of the witness. The note of hysteria is unnecessary, if only because the world can always be relied upon to bring the Christian into a state of affliction without his seeking it.

Yet in the light of our recent history we must distinguish between normal and abnormal situations, between a relatively tolerable life of sane institutions and, what Barth calls, 'isolated conflagrations'. The distinctively Christian affliction is more glaringly evident in the latter, but it never fails to be felt in the world's constant No to the Gospel and the Spirit. The world's hatred is the variable of Christian existence and exposes its vulnerability. The community of the risen Christ must come into collision even with the 'normal' world, for the Cross is implanted in the heart of our historical being.

Our curiously ambiguous reaction to suffering belongs to Christian existence in the world and adumbrates discipleship as an index of its reality. On the one hand we shrink from pain and repudiate with horror the innocents' ordeals; on the other, we venerate the glory of the faithful who would not alter their course of endurance. We thus come to apprehend in ourselves several spheres of suffering which must be integrated if a spiritual victory is to be won.

A reconciliation with the world on its own terms of secularization spells out certain defeat, whereas liberation from the world must now be seen as the goal of the witness in his spiritual struggle with the mechanics of existence. In this tremendous process of re-birth suffering comes not as an accident but as the inevitable pangs which bring in the new life.

At this point, however, the prophetic witness can no longer contest the destructive malice of historical power. He cannot actualize the re-birth of the world. Words fail him, signs are suppressed. The regeneration in Christ can, therefore, be never exhausted in prophetic terms but must be complemented in the priestly oblation. The prophetic witness lays down his life, as did Jesus on earth; the royal priest consummates the death of the prophetic spirit, as does Christ in heaven.

This mystical principle does not offend the realistic criterion of Auschwitz, for it acknowledges that the evil and nothingness to be fought is not only of this world but beyond history. Regeneration demands, therefore, not only a prophetic witness here and now but also the victory over the whole mystery of evil, which Auschwitz depravity has laid bare within history. The penetration of this historical evil leads to the uncovering of the dark and destructive spiritual 'devil' which prevails even over the prophetic witness.

The priestly office crowns the prophetic vocation in the final encounter with evil. We return to the Biblical tradition which at the outset transmitted, and depended upon, the priestly-prophetic unity and which through Christ was sealed with cosmic authority. The Son of Man is Son of God in his priestly-prophetic Person, for he who proclaims the Kingdom of God is the Son who makes intercession to the Father by offering his work. The celestial Christ is the eternal High Priest of mankind whose prophetic word and action come to fruition in self-oblation.

The pattern of priesthood answers thus to the problem of prophetic weakness, and especially the death of the prophets in their witness. It bestows inalienable rights and dignity to the witness and takes his regeneration beyond the contingency of events and the power of Anti-Christ. Yet this pattern also presses now, in the light of our experience, for a definition of priesthood in realistic terms.

This priesthood is obviously no longer an inherited privilege, but it still operates within the community which desires to stand against the world for the freedom of the Spirit. It is the office which ritually, inwardly, and ascetically shares the dying and rising of Christ.

The ritual of this priesthood must not be confused with ceremonies, for, as is well known, Auschwitz allows of no such helps, except very rarely and secretly, since neither bread nor wine are available for the proper celebration of the Last Supper. There are no outward trimmings to help the priest to maintain his priesthood. He cannot be vested, nor can he wash himself into the state of ceremonial purity. The exercise of his priesthood must, therefore, be mediated through its essence, objectively ordained and sustained by the Holy Spirit.

Through this divine 'clothing' the man is lifted out of the pressure of historical horror and comes to represent the ancient lineage of sacrificial giving. For him, therefore, dying and rising is not a verbal theme, but something which he enacts. As we saw, Jesus does not discontinue his priestly function on the Cross, but rather fulfils the whole prefiguration of oblation and sacrifice. In terms of Auschwitz this means that the way to the chambers of destruction is a priestly possibility. Thus we get out of the impasse of defeat by the world. The priest does not commit suicide, nor does he bow to his murderers because they are stronger than he, but he conquers them in as much as he sees himself, and those around him, as fulfilling the ancient deep theme of destruction. He enacts the event as a priestly ritual, without mitre, alb, stole, badge of office—after the order of Melchizedek.

This priesthood persists and resists its negation through inward perfection. The priesthood of Edith Stein reminds us, if it were necessary, that such a priesthood is of the hierarchy of the spirit, and therefore goes beyond the tribal Aaron-Levi conception and clerical, male exclusiveness. It is a secret priesthood, anointed by the life given willingly after the ascent of purgation, illumination, and union. Such a priesthood is the effect of regeneration and transforms the tragic reality into a God-affirming mystery.

The transformation can be summed up in the ancient purpose of all priesthood: Holy to God. Through the exercise of this priesthood the misery of human perdition is turned into homage to God. In the general setting of cursing the priest carries about the blessing. Though conditioned himself by the situation his powers are real.

He mediates the other world of compassion. When he lifts up his hand, addresses his fellows as a father, forgives them and strengthens them, he acts sacramentally. His actions and words betoken the very reality which the circumstances deny. His very existence is a re-enactment of the timeless service of mankind to God, and God's ever-present graciousness among men. The incantation of the name of God, the recitation of ancient prayers and liturgical texts, especially the Psalms, give the link not only to the past where God marched with his people but also to the future when he raises them from death.

This priestly function changes in intensity, but not in kind, under the conditions of Auschwitz. It breaks beyond the rules of normal synagogue and church order. It loses its special ecclesiastical support and its clerical status. Yet the sacerdotal function is still essentially that of mediation, receiving from God and giving to God. Therefore the priest's powers still depend upon the fulfilment of the obligations without which priesthood is not thinkable. The priest must be what he is appointed to do: the mediator only can mediate. Auschwitz stresses the by no means new truth that this demand involves a reasonable service of detachment and consecration. In this the priestly sufferer stands over against the lay community which even at the gates of death cannot and will not abandon its worldliness. His attitude is not one of superior condescension, but of identification and intercession. It is in the priest's power to impart through himself the gifts of God. In the face of death, above all, there is entrusted to him the ministry of reconciliation and consolation. He may speak of life and may administer sacraments of life and absolution to make peace in the midst of hell. His hands are made to hand on this ancient blessing and assurance.

We do not lack such examples of an inward priesthood brought to perfection. This priesthood dispenses with ecstasy as the heart of religious experience. Its continual training relies on ordered prayer and ascetic practice. The Rabbis, though formally not priests, pointed the way to attainment by the study of sacred scripture. Leo Baeck typified at Theresienstadt, during the period of torment and after the liberation, the serenity of priestly character achieved by life-long consecration. The recitation of sacred liturgies and texts, together with meditation and contemplation, signpost the path to priestly perfection. The inward conquest of self goes hand in hand with this training, which involves a reasonable detachment from the things of this world and a close attachment to the things of God.

The priestly ideal uses and converts the nothingness which the world of Auschwitz offers. Here the priest's sacerdotal dedication encounters the vacuum with self-sacrifice. The marvellous dignity of the priestly status is paradoxically the result of self-giving. The priest at the camp counts because he has no desires of self-importance and gives life because he stands already beyond extermination. He is the exact opposite to the king-rat. The hour of darkness cannot take him by surprise, since he has practised silence in darkness.

This self-consecration to God is not to be confused with an act, or acts of, self-laceration. It does not deny the goodness of the creation, for it affirms the Creator in the acceptance of suffering. The priest's humiliation under conditions imposed, and not chosen by him, is his supreme act in the glorification of God Creator. Whereas in 'normal' conditions he offers gifts—taking what is given—he now fulfils the 'sacrifice of praise' in giving his own self. Therefore it pertains to his office to make Eucharist even in hell, thus transforming, not the place, but its inmates into a free people of God.

The 'kingdom of priests' stands in complete contrast to the world of Auschwitz and modern secularism. By evoking a society, whose character and purpose is the likeness to God, it exalts dignity and honour among men against the brutalization through indignities and dishonour. It brings to the regeneration of men a supernatural wisdom which expresses itself in learning and art. Even in the camps there was never wanting an attempt to retain the dignity of man by satisfying his need for knowledge. The priestly contribution is the sacred knowledge, theology itself, pursued to maintain a constant state of sanctity. This theology, however, is no longer an academic study but the mental content of sacrificial living offered to God through Christ. Thus the chaotic, self-seeking society is converted through its priestly identification into a 'people', a well-co-ordinated building of precious stones erected on the chief corner stone, Christ the Priest.

This achievement of a spiritual hierarchy in a world conditioned by spirit-rejecting material power relies upon the indwelling of God's Spirit, received by the elect in disciplined love. The long ascetic tradition, therefore, stands wholly vindicated in this tragic age. We are not so much concerned here with the soldier's training and the advantages accruing to such as have hardened themselves for the race, for it is obvious that to endure hunger, thirst, hardship, lack of sleep, cold, etc., men and women must be trained to steel themselves against privations. The place of mortifications in the life of the Spirit goes beyond physical training. It opens the doors to union with God in a life of contemplation which has already seen through the emptiness of sin to the light of God.

The abandonment of riches, honour, fame, and sensual enjoyments enables the soul to be born anew. It is the active part of the priestly consecration whereby the new life enters. The fire of love spiritualizes and refines man in the fellowship of sacrifice. But this un-selfing is, despite the afflictions, always found to be a happy enterprise, if only because it represents an act of spiritual freedom.

Edith Stein in her work on St. John of the Cross, written before her deportation and salvaged, though left incomplete,[1] describes the soul's escape from the darkness of the night and its transformation into permanent love. She insists with prophetic insight on the reality of the 'wounds of love' in transformation. The priestly oblation is the manward aspect of the mystical union, but its perfection is the gift of God in the life after death. When 'my beloved is to me, and I to him' the soul enters an entirely new state beyond its own understanding. But even before the final consummation the soul experiences its mortification not as affliction but as the transition between betrothal and marriage. The deep descent into God comes before the final ascent. This poetical imagery, however, never obscures the fact that the Cross must be implanted in the heart, for 'the decisive factor is not doctrine, but the life.' The transformation of the soul is

[1] E.T. *The Science of the Cross*, 1960.

not an academic wilfulness, but the perfection of love in the immensity of God.

Edith Stein typified in her frail person the Jewish and Christian reply to Auschwitz, because it was given to her by God to implant the Cross in the complete desert of hatred. As one who awaited beatific perfection in profound peace she was completely prepared for the meaningless hell of perpetual destruction. The works that have been done in her name since 1945—and, of course, in the names of others like her—are evidence not only for spiritual achievement but also for immortality and consummation. The mystic's victory and intercessory power are seen to have surmounted wires, gassings, and burnings, in the aureole of eternal glory.

A REJECTION OF COMFORT

Resurrection and Ascension evoke a note of triumph. Our aim so far has been to relive the torments of the dead in order to bring redemption to the living. Since 'our image of man must forever include the hell which was their last experience on earth'[1] we endeavoured to include this image in a plea for reconciliation and hope. Yet the reader, while perhaps sympathizing with this attempt to appease the demons of the past, may be almost forced to reject the argument in the light of history and experience since Auschwitz. He may judge that it is only the past which can ever be redeemed thus, namely by liturgies and words of comfort. When the event is over and we look at it in retrospect we may perhaps theologize and subtly change the meaning of history, even if we could not touch history at the moment of occurring events. But actual history seems to demolish the theological presuppositions. Categories such as atonement and sacrifice, without which Auschwitz stands unredeemed, play no part in the making of what concerns us now.

This critique of the Christian interpretation of history, and particularly of our history, hits us all the more because we cannot relinquish our hold on history. It

[1] Erik H. Erikson, *Insight and Responsibility*, 1966, p. 85. The author battles very successfully with the abiding psychological problem of the camps.

surrounds us now, as the fences surrounded the hapless doomed. This history is not the academic thing which induces scholars to entertain a variety of theories about what may, or may not have, happened. Its realism is more destructive than any amount of quibbling about Biblical data.

The liberation from Auschwitz is itself symbol of the power of historical event. It was not taken by Michael and his angels, but rather by the Soviet forces. Hitler would never have been defeated by the Western allies alone. If, therefore, the Communist armies are to be equated with the ungodly we cannot help concluding that the devil is driven out by Beelzebub.

The opening of the camps had none of the romance associated with victory over evil. Little enough of life was left, and the liberators were tired men from afar off. The guilty, where found, were executed. The survivors were given a chance to return to life. In this first act of rehabilitation allied soldiers showed occasionally great humanity. But the delicate operation of the mental rehabilitation of the survivors had found no place in the handbook of the allied armies. Even the United Nations assumed that a rescue operation which dealt with the physical needs of the prisoners would be enough.

Already in 1946 it became apparent that the physical problem of displaced persons could not be solved without authorization from above. The former host countries no longer existed as before the war; none desired a return of the lost. However reduced in numbers, they were a liability. The chaos of the after-war ruin threatened to engulf them in their camps. Yet charitable organizations took a hand in the emergency and saved many lives,

especially those of children. Compassion stands out in a
pitiless sequence of history.

Yet compassion could not solve the major problems
of the survivors, since they and their spokesmen wanted
not charity but a national solution. Against the background of the cold war between East and West, and the
coming partition of India, the Jews clamoured for the
implementation of the Balfour Declaration by the making
of the state of Israel. If in previous chapters we have
hailed the establishment of the new Israel as a symbol of
resurrection we must now acknowledge the terrible facts
which preceded the declaration of May 14th, 1948.
Before Ben Guiron could invoke the Rock of Israel a
drama had been played out, in which Jews, Arabs,
British, Americans, Russians and the United Nations
played a part at times despicable, at times comic, and
always in direct opposition to what we could call resurrection. It is a story of incompatible claims which
symbolizes the fate of the weak and the supremacy of
force.[1]

If the survivors of Auschwitz did reach Jerusalem at
length this was due not to the resurrection of Christ, but
to the successful manoeuvring of negotiators, the despair
of boat-loads of refugees, the terror of determined freedom fighters, the lack of organized enemy opposition.
When the climax came, morale without supplies would
have perished. In Palestine, as later in Cyprus, and all
over Africa, we see clearly the things 'in the saddle'
which we should have preferred to leave behind. The

[1] For the historical details see Christopher Sykes, *Cross Roads to
Israel*, 1965. Cf. especially the account of the Evian Conference of
1938 for its masterly portrayal of evasions.

anti-theological twist of the historical event emphasizes
the irrelevance, if not the hindrance, of innocent goodness. In the clash of interests a good case is made good
by the force it can command.

The world after Auschwitz may have become sensitive
to the horrors of mass-extermination, but the principle
of state-craft has not, and could not have been, abated.
Power is the genuine representative of the communal
life of the human race, now brought to a fine point by
technical innovations. It steam-rollers into absurdity the
theological claims of salvation, resurrection, and regeneration. Against the vast back-cloth of power, such
parochial tokens of compassion as religious and other
organizations may offer, hardly deserve a historian's
glance. In decision-making events the so-called conscience of the human race is baffled by the complexity of
its struggling parts. The future of the whole lies beyond
its understanding.

The norm of life after Auschwitz is possibly less
demonic and more scientific than that of the age of the
dictators, but, even if true, this improvement is not a
theological achievement nor a state of affairs congenial
to Christian hopes. The present secular hope lies in the
controlled manipulation of power. The 'normal'
optimum is the absence of outrages, the operation of
mechanical processes. This norm inevitably controls the
human condition. The giant computer symbolizes the
subtle relationship between man the controller and man
the controlled. The rules of its game are wholly opposed
to the theological premises of the freedom of the Word,
the value of sacrifice, and the independence of Wisdom.
Since regeneration is unthinkable apart from the

prophetic-priestly creativeness in freedom the historical present would seem to crush the spirit as Auschwitz had done.

This defeat of the spirit is made more palatable by concessions of freedom which the secular society can afford to offer itself. The daily round of entertainment and sport belongs to the totalitarian pattern of life and grants an illusion of individual freedom. It acts as a substitute for the transcendental creativeness which compels man to seek liberation from the horror of mere existence.

The triumph of the secular hope is to be found, not in the things themselves, but in the welcome extended to the new totalitarian compulsion by mankind. The new positivism sanctions the secular delusion up to the hilt. It resembles the German corporate will, which, as R. Gray has shown,[1] judged before and after 1933 that an irresistible movement such as Hitler's was its own vindication. Its dynamism was considered self-authenticating. There are certain events in history, so the argument ran, which stand above moral evaluation. They have to be acknowledged, simply because they happen and because they work well. Excesses have to be overlooked in the face of such greatness. This positive assent to things and events is a spiritual decision of the first order and paralyzes the prophetic will and priestly work.

This popular siding with the inevitable trend stems from the nature of man himself. As long as he must seek

[1] *The German Tradition in Literature, 1871–1945,* 1965. Gray argues that this strange and highly persuasive positivism pervaded German culture before Hitler was ever heard of.

the gratification of his instincts and secure his position, his historical role must be opposed to the creation of spiritual freedom. But whereas in the past the human condition still found considerable territories free from such determination the age of the monolithic society leaves no loopholes for a life outside its orbit. It is pressed into a continuous development which is deemed 'natural' because it happens.

The enslaved spirit identifies right with might, for it acknowledges the historical process to be proper and necessary. All its moral judgments are explanations and extenuations of the natural process of events. Thus the makers of Auschwitz plead 'obedience to duty' to whitewash mass-murder, and the passive spectators offered no resistance in view of their obligations as citizens, parents, good comrades, etc.

Modern ethical theories illustrate the erosion of moral conviction, formerly based upon the freedom of the will. They go a long way towards justifying Auschwitz and preparing for another hell. They implicitly deny that the good is absolute, can be known, and may be done. No action can be commended on *a priori* grounds. Broad's academic dictum 'We can no more learn to act rightly by appealing to the ethical theory of right action than we can play golf well by appealing to the mathematical theory of the flight of the golf-ball'[1] is now seen in a different light, because born out by history. There is no authority for a categorical imperative but merely an analysis of possible courses of action.

Situations are relative to a variety of demands. Just as the prisoner at Auschwitz found himself in an

[1] Cf. the end of *Five Types of Ethical Theory*, 1930.

irrational situation in which the good was no longer attainable and in which the right was felt to be wrong, so the victim of modern situations no longer proceeds on the rational thesis that right action coincides with inherent goodness. We are guided by 'hunches' which attempt to make the best irrespective of right and wrong. By thus lowering our moral stature we reduce the element of freedom to a minimum of functional conformity. We arrive at the 'negative identity' of the genuine Auschwitzian type, guard and prisoner in one. The lost identity, the faceless crowd, the anonymous authority, derive from the by-passing of ethical concerns.[1]

The historical situation clearly precludes resurrection and ascension within its own terms of reality. But the historical situation may not achieve the final victory over Word and Spirit because, within the experience of Auschwitz, it exterminates itself in its destructive irrationality. It creates a situation of non-being which discloses the incurable sickness, the decay, and the stench of death. The apocalyptic nothingness awaits famine, which starves it to death, pestilence, which rots its institutions, and the sword, which escalates into the giant mushroom of burning.

[1] Ericson, op. cit. esp. p. 100: 'In order to lose one's identity one must first have one.'

XI

'WHAT THEN SHALL WE DO?'

THE EVENTS WHICH we have examined have led many of our contemporaries to capitulate to cynical inaction. But even responsible leaders restrict their actions and designs to a purely secular level. More remarkably still, many theologians subscribe to an ethic which confines action to man alone. Yet the historical situation with which we have to contend makes demands upon us of a transcendental kind.

The failure of theology has been and remains at the root of our enslavement. Its abstract terminology[1] could not prevent the great disaster which has figured so prominently in these pages. Words alone cannot save the victims from extermination and ethical judgments *without power* cannot break down the encircling barriers. Yet contemporary theology is still steeped in false conceptualization and many of its representatives imagine that the re-alignment of phrases can maintain the fabric of righteousness. In this world of make-believe the phrase is often mistaken for the deed. Thus a great victory is thought to have been won when a resolution has been passed. But the words of to-day resemble the meaning-

[1] In this respect Hamann, Kierkegaard and others were extraordinarily clear-sighted in uttering their protest before our time, but now, alas, their own words have become standard jargon in abstract clichés.

less babble 'qav-qav-tzav-tzav' which Isaiah ridiculed
in his time. Our abstract pretensions are as relevant to
our plight as were the tottering tipplers' sniggers to
Jerusalem decaying, besieged, and ready to fall.

The legacy of Auschwitz for theology is the return to
the rock of action against which hollow verbiage dis-
integrates. At Auschwitz itself there was little, or nothing,
left to be done—except the liberation of the camp from
outside. Its survivors look for liberation on a greater
scale. It derives from the Word which creates, sustains,
and perfects. This Word unites the doer and the act, for
by this Word we are not one thing and act out another.
It is the exact opposite of theoretical conceptualization
for it creates and sustains all things, beginning and end,
uniting men instead of dividing them. It uses words
sparingly and with precision. It is wary of ideals,
harangues, and demagogy. This eternal Word speaks
and asks: 'What shall I do for you?' and awaits our reply.
A reply to such an invitation cannot evade the main
issue: it will recapitulate in the most concrete manner
the acts of God and re-enact the saving history in our
midst. By its own question 'What then shall we do?' it
will act, invoking freedom in slavery and Grace in
meaningless existence.

The questioning reply 'What shall we do?' always pinpoints the concrete need of the moment, be it in battle or
any other crisis. It is the precursor to obedience or dis-
obedience, the realization of the absolute Either-Or, in
which all other distinctions vanish. In this question the
individual belongs to the community as a responsible
member without being swallowed up by totalitarian
claims. The one is identified with the many, the free

person with the gathered people, and he may say of past history: 'I also was there', identifying himself with the humiliations and triumphs of the suffering and rising 'We'.

The quest establishes thus a cosmic pattern of action and releases the questioner from the narrowness of a trivial concern. The whole Biblical dialectic enters into his concern because he enters it. He exists, and therefore acts, in a total historical dependence and in freedom beyond historical existence. Therefore his action may become meaningful.

As Abraham, the knight of faith (as Kierkegaard called him), moves into an alien world he transforms the political struggle of the moment into a blessing for all mankind. In his willingness to obey God, even to the extent of giving his only son, he becomes father of all. He fights, but his aims are peaceful; he builds, but what he could own he leaves to others; he is always on the move, leaving tokens of his presence everywhere. He is a mystic who acts realistically.

The patriarchal tradition bequeathes to us the rhythm of genuine action. It is tragic, but it is also successful. Isaac is bound, Jacob bereaved, Joseph sold and imprisoned; but Isaac is also restored, Jacob blessed, Joseph a provider of hungry nations. Similarly Moses, exposed, alienated, refugee, is called to lead a mob to freedom and lawful existence. All suffer and all finish well. This pattern of action and being is the warp and the woof of the loom of freedom in history. Hence the outcome remains unpredictable. Saul answers his 'What shall I do?' with witchcraft and suicide; David, humbled in his ecstasy, not only unites the tribes but leaves the stem of a tree, the dynasty which will reflect God's sovereignty among men.

Underlying the Biblical pattern of action in all its variety, God's scrutinizing 'What hast thou done?' meets mankind from the first. It is at once accusation and promise, a call to undo the past and to fashion the future. It is the prelude to God's 'Do this?', from which the people derive their 'This we will do'. In the community, which God ordains to give this assent to himself, freedom is contingent, but real. Here only it may be asked: 'What may and what can we do?', for here God does everything for the people: 'What more could I have done to my vineyard that I have not done?' This intercourse in faith is the origin and purpose of all free action. Israel, the naked baby, a bastard son, has been nursed all the time by God; washed, nurtured, clothed, and adorned by God, the servant nation has been told what to do: to act justly, to love mercy, and to walk humbly with God.

These concrete demands of faith establish the freedom of the divine society. When John the Baptist tells the people in answer to their 'What then shall we do?' to share their goods, demands of the tax gatherers to be scrupulously honest, and of the soldiers to refrain from violence and to be content with their pay, we may almost miss the point and take his answer to be another instance of hollow moralizing. But this is not so, for no man acts like that, and yet every man ought to act like that. The concrete demand does not exclude, but derives from, the supernatural. Similarly the lawyer who quotes the golden rule quite sincerely is not allowed to escape with verbal abstractions. Jesus insists on the decisive 'more', as told in the parable of the good Samaritan: 'Go, and do thou likewise!'

The pattern of faith-works is not merely humanitarian and pragmatic. In one story the food-storing farmer is shown to be a fool because he thinks he knows what to do, but forgets the proximity of death. In another story, a dishonest steward, who is 'resolved what to do' and succeeds in manipulating the bills, is mentioned with approval since he is at least aware of final accountability and its consequences. This pattern does not ignore death, and therefore does not die the death of a thousand qualifications. There are no 'works' in themselves apart from the transcendent faith, but there is equally no faith without the fulfilment of the commandment. The greater the 'must' of faith the greater the freedom of action.

The experience of Auschwitz stands within this pattern. The crisis of loss and death is ever-present, but within the compulsiveness of the historical situation there remains a degree of free decision. The total slave is also the free child of God who can act because he can respond. His activity is a response to having received the free gift of God. Similarly the jailors of Auschwitz, as Paul's jailor at Philippi, may be brought to the point of asking 'What must I do to be saved?' so as to be told 'Believe on the Lord Jesus Christ, and you shall be saved!'. The possibility of freedom in slavery is a spiritual act, in which everything that is done is first received. Thus the freedom of Auschwitz, too, must be wholly distinguished from any system of ethical duties. Its very concreteness derives from the transcendent freedom of the will without which liberation on such a scale cannot be initiated. Similarly our 'What shall we do?' is still-born even as a question unless it is lifted to the appropriate level of freedom, which is called faith.[1]

This self-transcendence is the concrete reflection of the divine Presence. Thus the Creator God is known in a thousand ways, just as the Redeemer and Sanctifier reflects himself on all levels of compassion and liberation. One piece of bread, one glass of water, may symbolize the highest degree of freedom attainable. On the other hand, institutionalized charity may choke freedom because it no longer reflects anything but its vested interest. When Tolstoy wrote his epoch-making 'What then shall we do?' (thoughts evoked by the census of Moscow) in 1886, he gave a crushing verdict on institutionalized charities and by his condemnation opened the path to revolution as an answer to the freedom-aspiring multitudes.

The criterion of action is not to be found in the smooth functioning of religious institutions. Indeed, the creative spirit is least likely to thrive in establishments tied up with property. The faith which restores sight to the blind and attempts the humanly impossible can only be hindered by a stake in the historical compulsiveness of things. The sad, or comic, spectacle of a religion, ecstatic in inspiration and liberating in purpose, which gets bogged down in the administration of cracking buildings, is a constant warning and, perhaps, also an inducement to action.

Our attitude to institutionalized religion provides not only the touchstone of our sincerity but also a test of our responsibility. An angry denunciation of all organizations is a poor response to the Word which requires continuity and works through traditional re-enactment.

[1] Cf. Tillich, op. cit., vol. 3, pp. 241 ff.

Edith Stein at Auschwitz is unthinkable apart from years spent at Carmel. Mother Maria in all her unconventionality requires the stability of orders. Thus freedom, as has often been observed, does not flourish in an aura of licence. On the contrary, the exercise of freedom flourishes against the background of settled and lawful institutions.

But this recognition does not give a charter to the perpetuation of institutions as such, especially when they are seen to fail in the liberation of the spirit. It is, for example, a sombre comment on the freedom of the spirit when economic necessity only succeeds in closing down unwanted plant. The present Word to the Churches calls for the pulling down, rooting up, trampling upon, and destroying of numberless institutions which are paraded as part of a sacred tradition without laying any genuine claim on them. They are freedom-restricting and tie up man's time and resources. They derive from the world of historical restrictions and no longer reflect the freedom of the Word. They prevent the prophetic spirit from planting and building its own expressions of reasonable utterance and recognizable service.

The mentality which cries for ever 'The Temple of the Lord' as an answer 'To what shall I do?' certainly finds plenty to do for idle hands, but it fails in the task of liberation. It is not the priestly side of religion, as is sometimes assumed. The oblation of self-giving to God by Christ in the Spirit requires no man-made temples. Indeed, they often stand in the way of the priestly office of reconciliation. The mentality which never escapes from the here and now achieves little in the here and now. It fails to bring even to secular institutions a whiff of freedom since every self-perpetuating office repudiates the transcendence of the spirit. Institutionalism as such is salt without savour. But institutionalism as a home for charismatic creativity aspires towards God's pattern of action and stands over against the world.

The old problem of the Kingdom and the world, or of Israel and the heathen, or of Church and State, has become more acute and complex with every passing century. If Augustine ultimately failed to relate the two worlds—and thereby yet made his greatest contribution to both the City of God and the city of this world—it is improbable that we shall succeed in our day. Auschwitz has, however, enabled us to see that whilst the earthly city may become, as the prophets and the gospels perceived, a veritable hell, our condemnation of this hell does not imply a withdrawal from the world. Similarly the apparent glories of the state in welfare and education and the abundance of material goods must not be taken as the forerunner of the Kingdom of God. The two worlds remain distinct, and a secular Christianity is a contradiction in terms. The secular world succeeds because it owns no power but its own. The kingdom stands against the world since it repudiates its power and its glory. But men belong to both worlds and discover in their dual role the inevitable conflict. We must 'do' in this present world, even within the framework of its institutions, though we have here no abiding city. We act here in the light of what we are to become. We endeavour to sow humane feelings and build humane institutions because they attest the spiritual worth which the world does not know and without which it devours itself.

But the true humanist must not lose himself in the world and sanction the world's doings. Unless he opposes its 'let us eat and drink' policy the world will assume that his consent condones its total claims. True humanism takes its authority from outside the given situation. What was and is needed is an authority for humane action which lies outside all contingencies. This is the eschatological spur to rebel against inhumanity and to affirm the transcendent possibility of freedom. The denial of the nihilistic, impersonal, all-enslaving tyranny must be heard and acted out before the corresponding Yes may be asserted. Yet this in-the-world-involvement with its out-of-the-world detachment is not an evasion, for it brings the eternal down to impinge upon concrete and departmental concerns.

Real humanity, offered 'in solidarity with the world, but not in conformity',[1] is not an ethical plaster to cover up a few unsightly offences. It is the new thing, the transcendent possibility of freedom. As the book of Deuteronomy insists, it is very near and not an esoteric extra. But it is not the good life simply, in the sense in which Plotinus defined it for many generations to come: 'If any man seeks in the good life anything beyond itself, it is not the good life he is seeking.' The life of Grace both comes from beyond anything this life can offer and aspires to an eternal consummation which lies beyond death. This eternal target can easily be abused by the specification of rewards and punishments, but however repulsive eschatological blackmail may appear, our actions are governed both by motivation and expectation. The theme of the sowing and the harvest cannot be

[1] K. Barth, CD, IV/3, p. 762.

removed from the re-making of life in bondage. Without the eternal perspective our enslavement reaches the proportions of Auschwitz, which Luther seems to have foreseen in his honest, but unattractive warning: 'If you believe in no future life I would not give a mushroom for your God . . . do then as you like; for if no God, then no Devil, no hell . . . ; then plunge into lechery, rascality, robbery, and murder.'

We become human by reacting to our existence in time as eternal creatures or children of God. We are human when we transform chaos into order, use impersonal machinery for personal ends. We articulate our humanity when we utter a decisive No to Auschwitz and all forms of scientific slavery and extermination, and a decisive Yes to the creativity of the spirit. Action is, therefore, not confined to physical activity, but to all total endeavours of transformation. Such actions of transformation may occur anywhere, but are most regularly encountered in the Auschwitz situation of dire peril. Healing, release, liberation, rehabilitation are mere words which bring out the contemporary parallels to Biblical acts of salvation. The connection stresses the moment and worth of transformation as the essential disclosure of the divine in man. It also warns us against confusing any such action with the rich man's largess who can draw on reserves of capital. The humanization in question springs from poverty and inner need.

After Auschwitz we understand the paradox that the giver needs to be given and that healing comes only from those who have been healed. Organized aid can soon get bogged down in an impersonal routine of feeding and healing; no transformation ensues. It stands in need of the Franciscan reminder that it is the mendicant who can afford to be most generous. This penitential approach agrees with the doctor's insight that he is useless as a mere conveyor of drugs and the applier of surgical techniques. He stands alongside his patient and is himself transformed by his humble identification. This treatment of sickness and need by participation, and the readiness of the psychologist to be healed, give the medical answer to our quest. It confirms not only the true relationship between healer and healed but utters the possibility of self-transcendence.

Therapeutic action without the penitential basis cannot be liberating. Without a transcendent orientation it cannot succeed. If the world be ultimately the absurd prison, which Sartre depicts in *Huis Clos*, healing is but a prolongation of agony. Healing demands an end. The cessation of guilt and the liberation of man by a valid transference open this perspective. Therefore every completed act of genuine healing shines like a star on the firmament.

In this field we are only at the beginning of a vast new enterprise in which group-therapy must play an ever-increasing part. It works on the proper principle that I am my brother's keeper and he mine. It must, however, heed the grave warning from Auschwitz, the *locus classicus* of insanity, that insanity lies, more often than not, within the group itself, and that sin and guilt are not shifted by the mere sharing of them. The truism that no-one can redeem his brother must militate against the extreme enthusiasm of group therapy. Even therapeutic action must be centred in atonement.

The priestly office and work, as we have seen in our

analysis of regeneration, fulfils this function. It is not at all surprising that many clinical specialists welcome the dedicated priest who is not, and does not wish to be, a welfare officer. The secularization of the sacred person misconceives the task of reconciliation. The true interpretation of healing stresses the distinctive function of patient, doctor, and priest. To the last falls the responsibility of actualizing the atoning power which the Holy Spirit makes available to all by each.

The relationship between these functions is the outstanding parable of responsible action. The re-enactment of God's work culminates in healing and forgiveness as realized in transference. This mysterious work of expiation goes beyond purely medical categories. It answers to man's conflict with himself, his striving after, or refusal of, liberation. Since I am potentially the guard at Auschwitz, I am the patient in this drama; because I am potentially the victim inside the camp, I look for the healer. Since I wish to go outside I require priestly blessing.

This conception of reconciliation goes beyond minimum aims. We are not concerned with the return of sick people to work or the reunion of divorcees. Liberations of this kind are short-lived. Even the liberation from Auschwitz, in the first place a release from squalor and cruelty, had to be a first milestone in a long pilgrimage. The integration of man, be he oppressor or victim, is no longer enough in itself. The healing of man in society is our immediate concern, but the immediate concern is meaningless without the ultimate concern, and, as stressed before, the temporal cannot be enterprised unless there beckons the eternal vista of man made

perfect in God. The action comes to be seen as sub-
servient to the agent who carries it out and for whom it
is done. The 'We' in our question takes command of the
impersonal 'Do', seeing that the former is potentially
eternal, and the latter is not.

Yet the radical experience of Auschwitz cannot support a purely subjective ethic in which personal considerations alone count. There are particular situations
in which even well-meaning forces cannot defeat the
giant forces of destruction and encompass the rights of the
individual. After Auschwitz it may be said that all other
ethical problems derive from this insoluble impasse. It is
a lesson of despair which had to be learnt during the war
when traditional freedoms had to be violated. For
example, the dilemma of the Swiss Government then
met the tragic givenness of the situation in that had it
admitted all the Jewish refugees who might have crossed
the border to safety it would have imperilled this very
safety since a German invasion would certainly have
followed.[1]

Hence we must reluctantly oppose the presumption of
what has become known as 'situation ethics'.[2] Here the
attempt is made to regulate conduct not according to
objective principles but with reference to 'calculated
love'. Whilst we agree that the person outweighs in
importance any action we cannot reduce the scope of

[1] This is not always recognized, especially among the most con-
scientious of the Swiss, who imagine that a fear of reduced rations
dictated this admittedly repulsive measure.
[2] Cf. Joseph Fletcher, *Situation Ethics*, 1966. The author is typical
in his use of 'love' as a real counter in the moral system, and not as
its supreme problem.

action to such a nebulous concept as love. Even before mob anarchy became mob government Dean Inge stressed that 'Love of God is talked about more often than felt.' The same is certainly true of human love, which does not normally control conduct, if only because real life favours aggression and does not present us with a community of interest. The situation, therefore, generally contradicts the factor which is meant to regulate it.

Clinical research pricks the bubble of situational love-ethics, for it confirms the prophetic analysis of our sickness. It is an affront to reason and experience to shelve the problem of love by playing a false trump-card, such as 'Love God—or man—and do what you like'. Even the support of a few Biblical texts cannot alter the fact that we cannot love as we would and that our inability to love is text-book stuff in every clinical log-book. The Auschwitz shadow pursues us everywhere in the obsessional blindness of eyes and deafness of ears which seek release in destruction, and not in love. Violence is not an isolated phenomenon. Many, if not all, want it, openly or secretly, occasionally or always. It gives them the pleasure which love, the unattainable, fails to induce. We therefore argue in a circle if we commend love as the main-spring of action, when love—even if well-defined as an attitude of the will—is yet to be won by healing.

This confession of failure connects with the heart of our particular problem which the Hitler type of patient always sets. He scorns the very idea of healing and solves his psychosis in the to him far more acceptable and time-honoured fashion of 'determining to be a villain'. He laughs at the restrictions of the vocabulary of moralizing

love. Given no objective law, and no express image of the
transcendent Man, he wins, or thinks he does.

Far from denigrating love we elevate it as the transcendent principle which authenticates personal action.
The need for, and the deficiency of, love point to the
divine order where our subjective approximations are
objective fact. Only thus are we in a position to counter
the blunt 'We will enjoy ourselves in destroying everything by hatred' with a valid affirmation of humanity
itself.

This critical estimate of our status and our powers by
no means implies a defeatist quietism. Love objectified
does not lessen its existentialist availability. Love transcendental does not confine itself to metaphysical spheres
and laws. The whole law-love controversy is bedevilled
by a prejudicial belief that we can divide reality in this
way. But we know enough about ourselves to realize that
we do not act by having one foot in legalism and another
in that of *agape* or unselfish love. The real problem
always concerns the possibility of stimulating, authen-
ticating, and eternalizing our relationships in such a way
that they are transcendent in their significance and
duration. Though the erection of a system is manifestly
impossible the delineation of an objective hierarchy of
love validates our intentions.

The Apostolic church did precisely this. It regarded
love as the apex of human behaviour and the consummation of all striving. But it did not neglect the practice
of lesser virtues and recited, it would seem, lists of
virtues, which were not unknown among the pagans.
But the apostolic edge to the recital was the identification
of all perfection with the Messiah whom God has raised

from the dead. Thus the virtues were no longer seen as abstract codes. The possibility of justice, brotherliness, compassion, purity, goodness, fidelity, etc., was found in the objective covenant situation into which men were drawn by God himself.

Needless to say, the lists varied from place to place, and distinctions were allowed between the relative merits of virtues named. In a hierarchical structure the lower passions must be made to agree with our highest aspirations. Thus our natural aptitudes of mind and body were given a valid place within an ideal world where nothing was lost. Acts of prudence, temperance, fortitude, and justice were hailed as cardinal virtues which overcome the known evils of folly, excess, cowardice, and injustice. But these virtues were not homeless layers straying in a morally chaotic universe, but brought to perfection by the faith in, the hope for, and the love in God.

The horrors of Auschwitz, past and future, by no means shake these foundations. On the contrary, they seem to demand a return to such an objective order. Given a pattern of this kind, and not otherwise, the process of outer and inner restoration can be validated. Put concretely, the electrified wire fencing—of the actual camp, its mechanism, and symbol of many institutions and our alienated self—is evidence for the necessity of a transcendent perfection within a spiritual hierarchy of values. This is the 'must' without which human life, let alone significant action, is impossible. Unless we prefer Auschwitz and act as the covenanters of death we must equate our yearning for freedom with an ascending scale of virtues.

The work of reconciliation, which is our primary

concern, becomes thus integrated into the cosmic whole and enables us to answer our pragmatic 'What then shall we do?' with God's transcendental 'This I will do'. In terms of Auschwitz this means that we begin with the washing of filthy clothes and delousing neglected children. We proceed to feed them as we feed ourselves. When they are with us facing the future of the over-populated planet the real work begins.

Reconciliation marks the ascent on the ladder to perfection. This ladder does not lead into a fastness of systems but to an ever-increasing realization of freedom in Grace. Freedom is not only the criterion of what we ought to do, but also the assurance of God's presence in our bondage. All acts of liberation reflect the God-in-Man freedom. The freed prisoner who advances in freedom is the answer to our quest.

The liturgical petition 'Libera nos . . .' sums up, in all languages, whether formally intoned or ejaculated as a cry from the heart, the re-enactment of God's trans-cendent will in the world. In this petition converge human need and desire and theological tradition. Transcendent action is its fulfilment.

XII

CONCLUSIONS

AT THE BEGINNING we stated our purpose of bringing together seemingly incompatible entities of thought. The speech about God was to be contrasted with the human condition, freedom with slavery. The former was meant to throw light upon the darkness which the latter has thrown around our historical existence. We may now summarize some results of our enquiry.

In seizing upon the most radical manifestation of enslavement we encountered the human condition at its most vulnerable. The unique horror of Auschwitz cannot be generalized but it discloses the potential perils of our social existence. It also articulates the need for rational treatment and a liberal openness to the many-sided causes of our sickness. A medicine to immunize ourselves against the deadly virus does not exist, but the courage to fight it is the certain prerequisite of human freedom.

The gulf between freedom and slavery is wide and cannot be bridged except by a special effort. Yet we had to use no eccentric artifice to relate our present-day burden to traditional ideas. The scientific norms of theology correspond to events, motives, and consequences in history.

The world in which we live brings to our consciousness scenes of delights and repulsion. Tragedy and pathos mingle with comedy and laughter. This variety of numberless reactions can and must be bent to certain rational norms to make sense. Primary events and feelings are to be seen *sub specie aeternitatis*. But the string of happenings and the discourse of revealed truth are uneasy bed-fellows.

Thus we ventured to examine the misery of Auschwitz as a reflection of an eternal reality. We used the awesome norms of sacrifice, atonement, and reconciliation in connection with suffering and murder. In this process of comparing and contrasting historical reality with theological terms we found the germ of freedom in self-giving and self-transcending. If we take the modern world at its empirical best and worst, without succumbing to its spell, we can detect intimations of transcendent freedom.

This method of speech counters contemporary nihilism and despair. At the same time it cannot be used as just another bit of propaganda, since it cannot proceed at all unless it is grounded in the truth. But this claim cannot be entertained apart from certain basic assumptions. It is only possible to find meaning in history if there is such a meaning to be found and if we can detect it. This means that we are encased in history and yet may stand outside our own history.

This belief cannot be proved but it may be suggested by certain analogies. In our subject, however, it was clear from the start that nothing like Auschwitz had ever happened before. There could therefore be no question of spotting identical happenings elsewhere. Complex historical events are in any case allergic to a simple method of explanation by identity. Analogies, however,

have a suggestive quality which frees these events from
their immediate happening.

Even in the twentieth century there are patterns of
behaviour in history which correspond, strongly or
weakly, to traditional norms. The grim realities, as well
as the more pleasing aspects of life, do not fall outside
their orbit of meaning. Thus the temporal world never
fails to disclose points of reality for those who are ready
to evoke and accept Biblical imagery. In that sense our
history still belongs to God's act in creation and redemption.

Our analysis of Auschwitz forced us to break down the
process and organization of extermination history. We
found there as little meaning as we find a core in a peeled
onion. Only when we removed layer after layer from
the impersonal history did meaning appear in Man. The
personal we now accept as the index of historical meaning. This commitment to personalism does not revert to a
form of individualism in which 'I exist' apart from historical pressure and scientific strata of reality. On the
contrary, in my involvement with biological necessity
and historical enmity I discover potential, contingent
transcendent possibility.

This possibility we may now equate with man's status
as a creature, created in God's image. It is a status which
harbours an infinite number of levels of significance. It
hovers between total annihilation and total fulfilment.
The decisive choice is freedom itself. To the extent that I
use, or disabuse, the freedom offered me in creative
accountability I rise above, or fall into, the trap of
totalitarian slavery.

Man occupies thus a unique place in the divine

economy. He is made to be like God, but never to be God. The doctrine of the divine superman died at Auschwitz, and with it anthropology as a disguise for theology. The self-exaltation of man and the definition of reality in exclusively human terms lead to the denial of freedom which obliterates the divine image.

The radical nature of modern experience almost despairs of a verbal definition of Deity. At Auschwitz the wholly Otherness of God, hidden and immense, no longer clashes with the disclosure of the One as near, loving, and afflicted in the afflictions of man. The science of the Cross gives a new edge to the infinite qualitative distinction between God and Man in its acclamation of the Creator of the Universe as the Lamb of sacrifice.

Salvation from slavery and for a free existence is thus grounded in the objective and cosmic work of God. Our realization of the cosmic import of the work of Christ enables us to recover the *raison d'être* of our historical existence. Auschwitz frees us from narrow religious and ecclesiastical grooves of thinking. It confronts the whole world with its guilt and the inescapable need for atonement. Legal arguments, moral concern, sacrificial images, and psychological need adumbrate the ancient theme of restitution and reconciliation. This objective view of the atonement with its realistic possibility lifts our liberation from the past out of its pernicious religiosity and trivial concerns. It opens the way to an eternal future.

This offer of expiation after Auschwitz presupposes that men, aware of their sickness, desire to be healed. In asking 'What then shall we do?' we met with the hard core of our problem, for we had to recognize that no action can be contemplated unless healing be accepted first. We found no answer for the deep destructive force which wills its own and everyone else's enslavement. Therapy marks the beginning of restoration because it spells out freedom to the not-free. But even the clinical interpretation and practical implementation of healing cannot compel the not-free to submit to Grace.

A therapeutical reading of the atonement cannot offer reconciliation—to God, to others, to self—as a cheap buy. It manifests the eternal paradox of freedom and of love. The most necessary and most desirable and best belong to Grace and are rejected by the Grace-less. But this paradox can now be seen as a liberating principle, for it condemns the things 'as they are' and illumines that which 'ought to be'. The nightmare of slavery must yield to the 'Other' which is not yet. This prophetic and apocalyptic insight ends the rule of mere diagnosis. It confronts healer and patient with creative theology.

But what is this theology? Certainly not the endless classification of religions and methodical criticism of ancient documents. There is not a breath of freedom in this routine syllabus of inherited, but irrelevant, questions. Nor can we advance by making a comfortable division between the pure science and its practical application. The whole discipline is under judgment until it stands consciously for a contemporary and militant freedom.

The old institutions by themselves are powerless to effect this end, but the spiritual forces which once built these institutions are alive to-day. Thus the legal codifications can be seen as aids to freedom, balancing the charismatic ecstasies of prophetic vision and apocalyptic enthusiasm, and both support and are sustained by the accumulated wisdom and reflection of the mystic. These are the freedom-carrying presences of God in the camp of slavery, torment, and extermination. They are the freedom-making, reconciling, and creative norms of Christ and Spirit in a free world.

Liberation is not a matter of words but of power. The act of remembrance sets forth not only our decision for freedom but releases the spirit of divine freedom in human bondage. Lamentations, confessions, petitions, intercessions, thanksgivings and jubilations create the forms which transform the camp of enslavement into the walls and towers of the Kingdom of God.

Libera nos, Domine. . . !